THE CHRONICLES OF NARNIA

Comprehension Guide
Written and designed
by Ned Bustard

veritas
PRESS

This book is dedicated to
my Friends of Narnia
from years gone by—

Miss Orlando
Stephanie Feeck
Diana Bauer
Jerusha Tiner

First Edition 2002

Copyright ©2002 Veritas Press
www.VeritasPress.com
ISBN 1-932168-02-8

Printed in the United States of America.

THE CHRONICLES OF NARNIA
Table of Contents

THE CHRONICLES OF NARNIA
How to use this Guide

This guide is intended to help you study, understand, and enjoy *The Chronicles of Narnia.* You might ask if a guide is really necessary to read a book. Is the student not just working to improve reading skills while being taught to enjoy reading a good book? Certainly, it is the case that the more a child reads, the more he should improve his skills, but quantity is not the only issue. Once a child has received adequate phonetic training he should learn how to read a book. Most educators using this guide will be teaching children in the grammar stage, generally understood to be during the elementary years in classical education. (For a thorough understanding of classical Christian education a reading of *Recovering the Lost Tools of Learning* by Douglas Wilson is highly recommended.) The basic goals of reading in the grammar stage are as follows:

The student should be able to:
1. Fluently read a given selection orally.
2. Show an increased desire for reading.
3. Show comprehension on a literal and inferential level.
4. Demonstrate an increased vocabulary.
5. Identify basic Biblical values in the literature being read.
6. Identify various styles (myths, poems, fantasy, fiction, nonfiction, etc.)

Answers to the questions are found in the back of the guide. The students' answers should be in complete sentences, and they should restate the question in their answer. The question of grading is one that always arises. You may assume that each question is worth five points.

Example:
Question: What had Digory been doing just before he met Polly?
Answer: Just before he met Polly, Digory had been crying.

THE CHRONICLES OF NARNIA
How to use this Guide

Such writing practice trains the student to answer thoroughly, completely, and with proper grammar. Another reason is to encourage integration. We want students to understand that how they write something is as important as what they write.

Narnia is a rich, magical land to visit. Teachers may wish to extend their time there. One possible approach would be to read *The Magician's Nephew* and *The Lion, the Witch and the Wardrobe* the first year then stretch the remaining books over the next several years. The questions and the projects are written in such a way that they could be used for older students, with older students expected to go into greater detail and depth in their answers. Teachers should also excercise their freedom in skipping some of the comprehension questions if they find they are too difficult or time consuming.

There are many materials that have been created about and around the Chronicles, including movies, radio dramatizations and commentaries. Paul F. Ford has created a marvelous book called *Companion to Narnia* which is both useful and entertaining to the Narnian afficionado. This comprehensive work contains alphabetically arranged and indexed entries covering all the characters, events, places, and themes that Lewis wove into his fictional world. It illuminates the philosophical, spiritual, and psychological significance behind each story, while explaining the symbolic and thematic threads that unify the series.

THE CHRONICLES OF NARNIA
History Cards Project

According to C. S. Lewis' timeline, Narnia lasted for 2,555 years between our history of the years 1888-1949 A.D.

Veritas Press has a flashcard program for studying history. An example of a flashcard is shown below. Each card has the name of the event and an illustration of the event on the front. On the back, the event is repeated along with the date. A summary of the event follows and the card number in the upper right hand corner keeps the events in sequence.

Photocopy the cards on the next two pages and fill one out for each Narnian book to summarize what happened. Then glue the two pages together to form each flashcard. The event titles should *not* be the name of the books. Name the event instead. For example, *The Magician's Nephew* would either be "Creation of Narnia" or the "Reign of King Frank I" and *Prince Caspian* would be "The War of Deliverance." There are many more events that could have flashcards made for them than just the seven books.

In addition to cards summarizing the *Chronicles,* flashcards could be written and illustrated for "The Telmarine Invasion," "Olvin of Archenland," and "King Gale and the Dragon," just to name a few. In the Appendix is a timeline which lists some of the other events in Narnian history. If you'd like to place the cards in sequence with the Veritas Press flashcards, the card numbers should fall between 282 and 290.

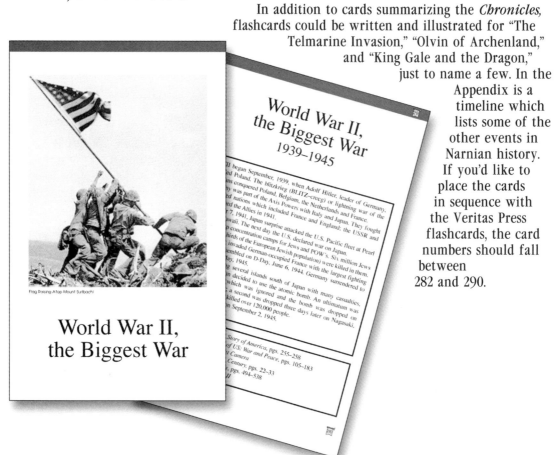

THE CHRONICLES OF NARNIA
History Cards Project

Image

Event

_____

_____

THE CHRONICLES OF NARNIA
History Cards Project

Card #

Event

Date

Who
What
Where
When

THE CHRONICLES OF NARNIA
Map of Narnia and the Surrounding Countries

THE MAGICIAN'S NEPHEW
Chapter 1—"The Wrong Door"

1. What characters from other books are used to set the time period for this first account of magical travels in *The Chronicles of Narnia?*

   _____

   _____

2. What had Digory been doing just before he met Polly?

   _____

   _____

3. What had Polly discovered behind the attic of her home?

   _____

   _____

   _____

4. Where were Polly and Digory trying to go when they set off exploring on that cold, rainy summer day?

   _____

   _____

   _____

   _____

5. What did Polly first notice in the sitting room?

   _____

   _____

   _____

6. Describe the person they found in the sitting room.

_____

_____

_____

_____

_____

7. What gift did Uncle Andrew give to Polly before she left his room?

_____

_____

THE MAGICIAN'S NEPHEW
Chapter 2—"Digory and His Uncle"

1. What was the first thing Digory did when Polly left the sitting room?

   _____

   _____

   _____

2. What was the name of Uncle Andrew's godmother and how does her name suggest evil?

   _____

   _____

   _____

   _____

3. What was physically remarkable about Uncle Andrew's godmother?

   _____

   _____

   _____

   _____

4. Where did the box Uncle Andrew was given come from originally?

   _____

   _____

   _____

   _____

5. Digory called Uncle Andrew "rotten" and an "evil magician." Why did this not bother Digory's uncle?

_____

_____

_____

_____

_____

6. What was the only way the rings would work?

_____

_____

_____

_____

THE MAGICIAN'S NEPHEW
Atlantis and Le Fay

Uncle Andrew alludes to two things in passing that students may wish to know more about. Following are two brief readings which teachers may wish to read to younger students and discuss or have their older students use as a springboard for deeper literary investigations.

Atlantis is a mythical island in the Atlantic, west of Gibraltar, that supposedly sank beneath the sea during a violent eruption of earthquakes and floods some 9,000 years before Plato wrote about it in his *Timaeus and Critias.*

The noble and powerful people of Atlantis possessed great wealth thanks to the natural resources found throughout their island. The island was a center for trade and commerce. The rulers of this land held sway over the people and land of their own island and well into Europe and Africa.

At the top of the central hill, a temple was built to honor Poseidon which housed a giant gold statue of Poseidon riding a chariot pulled by winged horses. It was here that the rulers of Atlantis would come to discuss laws, pass judgments, and pay tribute to Poseidon.

A water canal was cut through the rings of land and water running south for 5.5 miles to the sea. The city of Atlantis sat just outside the outer ring of water and spread across the plain covering a circle of 11 miles. This was a densely populated area where the majority of the population lived.

Beyond the city lay a fertile plain 330 miles long and 110 miles wide surrounded by another canal used to collect water from the rivers and streams of the mountains. The climate was such that two harvests were possible each year. One in the winter fed by the rains and one in the summer fed by irrigation from the canal.

Surrounding the plain to the north were mountains which soared to the skies. Villages, lakes, rivers, and meadows dotted the mountains.

For generations the Atlanteans lived simple, virtuous lives. But slowly they began to change. Greed and power began to corrupt them. When Zeus saw the immorality of the Atlanteans he gathered the other gods to determine a suitable punishment.

Soon, in one violent surge it was gone. The island of Atlantis, its people, and its memory were swallowed by the sea.

Morgan le Fay is, in Malory's *Morte d'Arthur,* Arthur's half sister, the daughter of Arthur's mother Igraine and her first husband, the Duke of Cornwall. She is also presented as an adversary of Arthur's: she gives Excalibur to Accolon so he can use it against Arthur and, when that plot fails, she steals the scabbard of Excalibur which protects Arthur and throws it into a lake. In *Sir Gawain and the Green Knight* she is presented as the instigator of the Green Knight's visit to Arthur's court, partly motivated by her desire to frighten Guinevere. Despite Morgan's enmity towards Arthur and Guinevere, she is also presented as one of the women who takes Arthur in a barge to Avalon to be healed. This view of Morgan as healer has its roots in the earliest accounts of her and perhaps to her origin in Celtic mythology. In the *Vita Merlini* (c. 1150) Morgan is said to be the first of nine sisters who rule the Fortunate Isle or the Isle of Apples and is presented as a healer as well as a shape-changer. It is to this island that Arthur is brought. Morgan proclaims that she can heal Arthur if he stays with her for a long time. Morgan is also said to be the wife of King Uriens and the mother of Yvain or Ywain. Morgan rarely appears in post-medieval works—until the twentieth century.

THE MAGICIAN'S NEPHEW
Chapter 3—"The Wood Between the Worlds"

1. Describe the place Digory ended up after placing the ring on his finger.

   _____

   _____

   _____

   _____

   _____

   _____

   _____

   _____

2. What did Digory and Polly see that made them remember where they had come from?

   _____

   _____

   _____

3. What from our world did Digory use to explain how the Wood worked in relation to other worlds?

   _____

   _____

   _____

4. What did Polly insist upon before she would consent to explore other pools?

   _____

   _____

   _____

   _____

5. What did Polly suggest that they do so they could find their way back to the home-bound pool?

_____

_____

_____

6. Uncle Andrew did not understand how the rings really worked. How did the green and yellow rings operate?

_____

_____

_____

_____

THE MAGICIAN'S NEPHEW
Wood Between the Worlds Game

A fast-paced game for 2 players.

Components:

gameboard
2 player pieces (Digory and Polly)
20 Pond cards
6 Green Ring cards
1 six-sided die

The Wood Between the Worlds is played on a 9x9 board, with most of the squares representing the forest but some squares representing ponds. The board is found on the following pages. It is recommended that the pages be photocopied onto thicker paper (for a larger gameboard, photocopy onto 11" x 17" at 130%), attached together with the E row overlapping, and the pools colored. There are a total of 21 ponds on the board, with the remaining 60 squares representing the forest.

The center square, E5, is the "correct" pond and is identified as such—Digory has left an arrow cut into the grass. This is the one players need to get to in order to return to their own world and win the game. (NOTE: There is no card for the pond at E5 in the Pond card deck.)

One player is Polly and the other is Digory. They begin the game on opposite corners of the board.

Each player begins the game with five green ring cards. If players find the game too easy, begin the game with three green ring cards. The 20 Pond cards are shuffled and placed next to the board face down.

The goal is for the players to reach the centermost pond square (E5) on sequential turns, with each player still having at least one green ring card.

The oldest player goes first. On a turn, a player rolls a six-sided die. After rolling a 1, 2 or 3, that player moves that number of spaces horizontally or vertically (or a combination of both), but not diagonally. It is permissible to cross the same space twice on a turn, and it is also permissible to finish a turn on the same space at which you began that turn.

After rolling a 4, that player jumps into a nearby pond (it makes no difference which one) and loses a green ring card. That player then draws a pond card from the top of the pile and moves to the pond listed on the card.

If a player rolls a 5 or 6, he forgets how long he's been in The Wood and must move one space away from the center pond. This movement must be horizontal or vertical; it may not be diagonal.

Any time a player steps onto a pond square (whether by choice, by rolling a 4, or because the player had to move away from the center pond due to a roll of 5 or 6), that player loses a green ring card, and must draw a pond card and move to the pond shown on the card. That player's next turn begins on the new pond.

To win, players must land on the center square on sequential turns, first one and then the other. Each player must have at least one green ring card remaining.

Players can freely exchange green ring cards to cooperate in getting to the middle. (Think of this as tossing the ring through the woods to the other player.)

Game concept and rules by Erik Arneson.

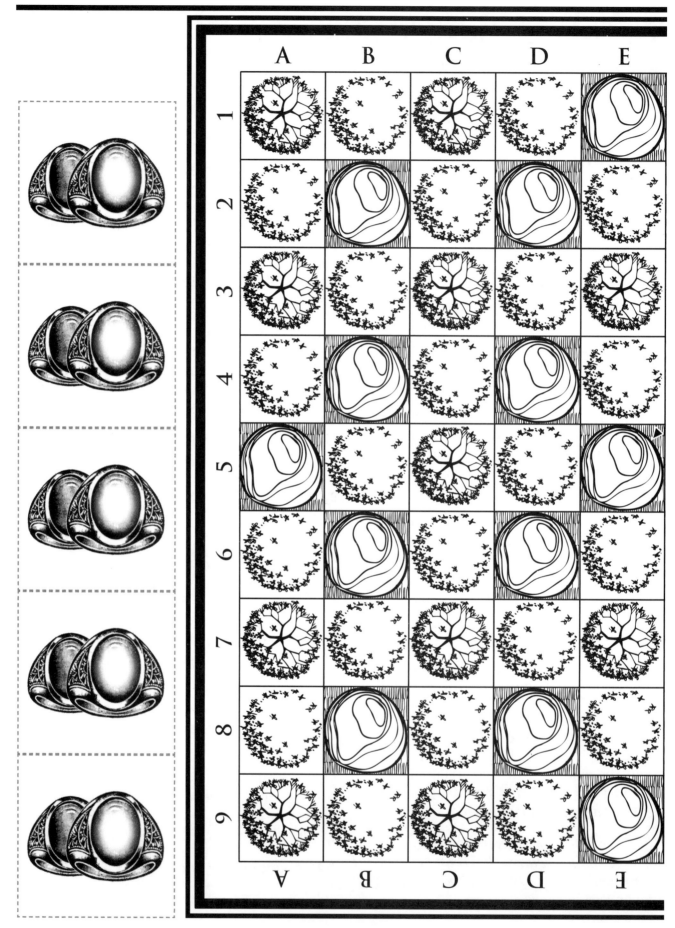

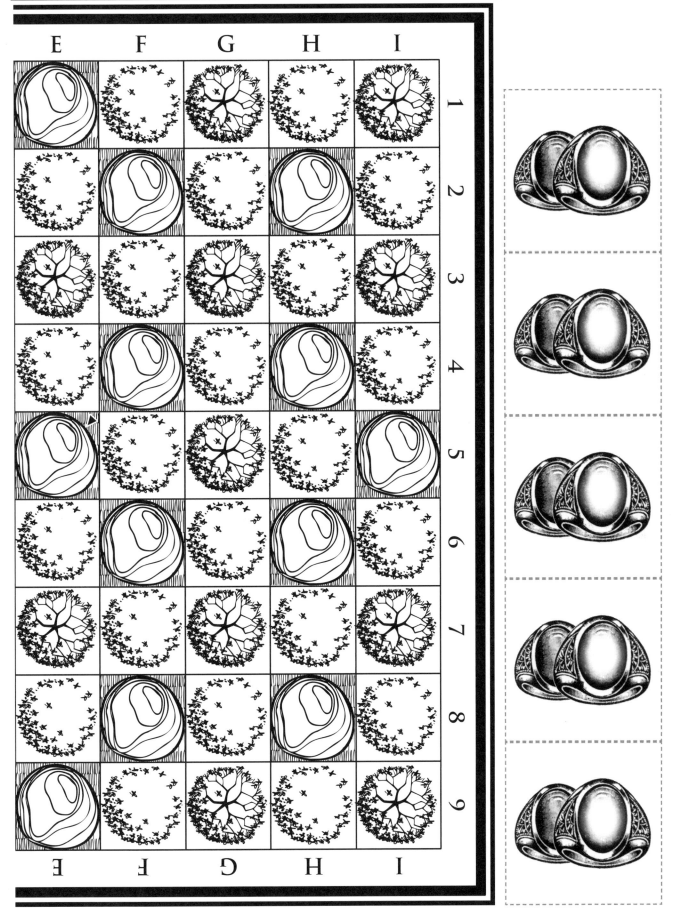

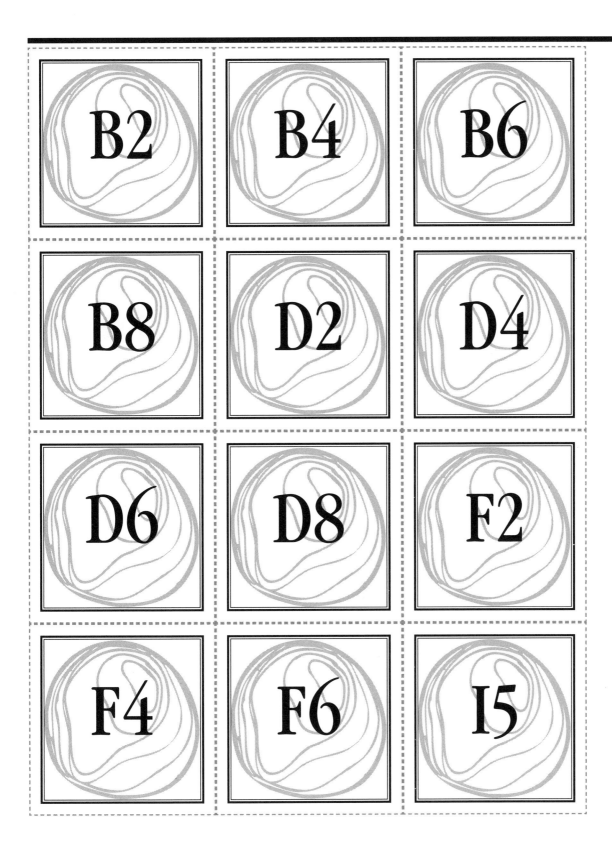

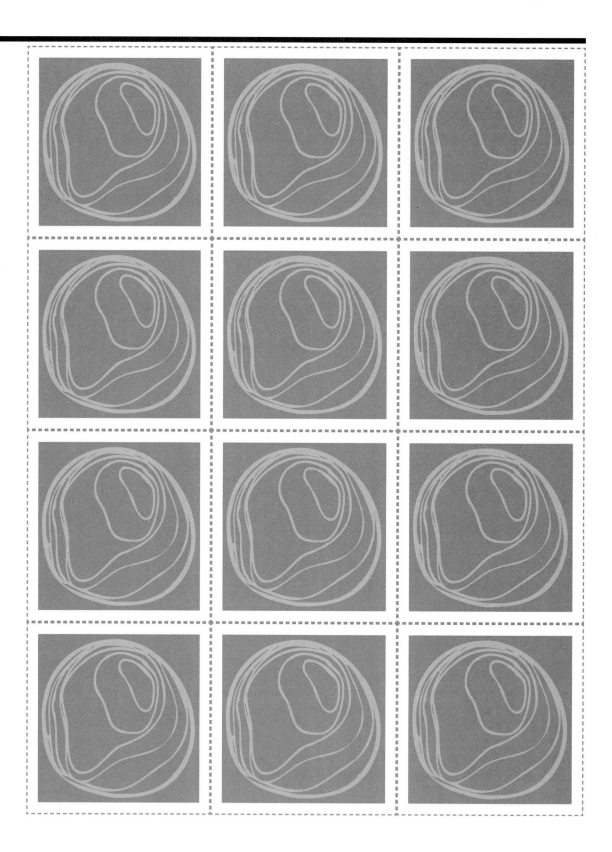

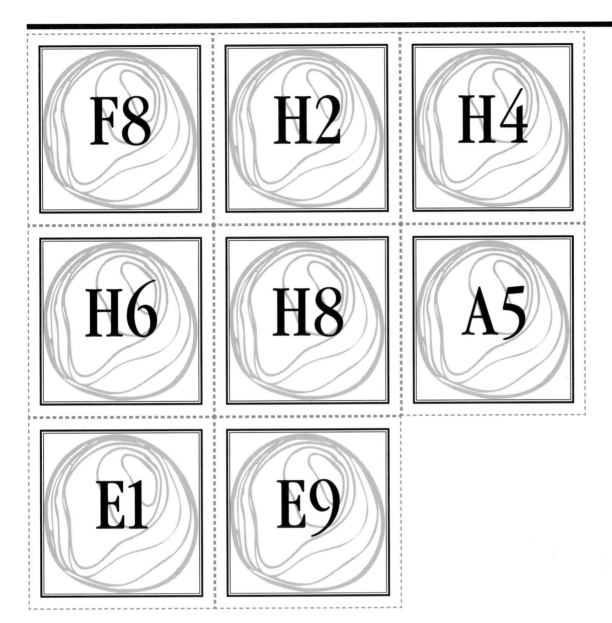

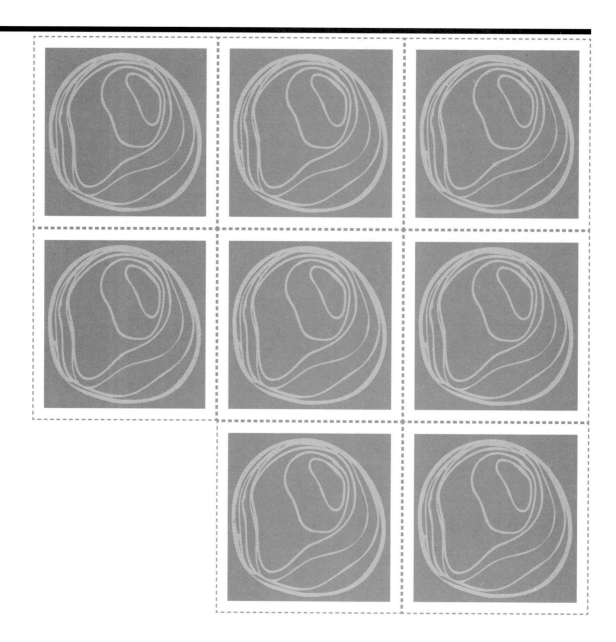

THE MAGICIAN'S NEPHEW
Chapter 4—"The Bell and the Hammer"

1. What was odd about the light in the world that the children visited?

   _____

   _____

   _____

2. In what one way was this world like the Wood Between the Worlds?

   _____

   _____

   _____

3. What did they notice about the elegantly dressed figures that they found as they walked down the row of them?

   _____

   _____

   _____

   _____

   _____

4. Describe what they found that had a message cut into it which began: "Make your choice, adventurous Stranger . . ."

   _____

   _____

   _____

   _____

   _____

   _____

5. Why did
    Digory and Polly
    have a quarrel?

    _____

    _____

    _____

    _____

6. After twisting Polly's arm away from her
    yellow ring, what did Digory do?

    _____

    _____

    _____

    _____

THE MAGICIAN'S NEPHEW
Chapter 5—"The Deplorable Word"

1. What happened when the bell was rung?

   _____

   _____

2. What sorts of things were pointed out to Polly and Digory on their "tour" of the castle?

   _____

   _____

   _____

3. How did Jadis defeat her sister?

   _____

   _____

4. When Digory and Polly questioned the Queen's actions against the ordinary people of Charn, how did the Queen respond?

   _____

   _____

   _____

5. What did the Queen wrongly assume about Digory's uncle?

   _____

   _____

   _____

6. How were the children finally able to reach the rings in their pockets?

   _____

   _____

   _____

THE MAGICIAN'S NEPHEW
Chapter 5—Project

The poem by the Golden Bell goes as follows:

Make your choice, adventurous Stranger;
Strike the bell and bide the danger
Or wonder, till it drives you mad,
What would have followed if you had.

Write another verse or two to the poem in the meter and style of the poem that would serve as a warning label against striking the bell. The "rest" of the poem could explain who set up the bell or what she had done and why it isn't a good idea to ring it.

_____

_____

_____

_____

_____

_____

_____

_____

_____

_____

_____

_____

_____

_____

_____

THE MAGICIAN'S NEPHEW
Chapter 6—"The Beginning of Uncle Andrew's Troubles"

1. How did the Queen, or Witch, follow Digory and Polly into the Woods?

   _____

   _____

2. What did being in the Woods do to Jadis?

   _____

   _____

   _____

3. When Jadis appeared in the sitting room she appeared extremely beautiful and big. What did some say was the reason for her great height?

   _____

   _____

   _____

4. What did Jadis request Uncle Andrew to obtain for her so she could see the city?

   _____

   _____

5. What did Jadis threaten Uncle Andrew with if he proved treacherous?

_____

_____

_____

_____

6. For what was Digory required to apologize?

_____

_____

_____

7. How did Uncle Andrew act "silly in a very grown-up way?"

_____

_____

_____

_____

8. How was Uncle Andrew planning to pay for entertaining the Witch in London?

_____

_____

_____

THE MAGICIAN'S NEPHEW
Chapter 7—"What Happened at the Front Door"

1. Where did Aunt Letty think Jadis was from?

   _____

   _____

2. What did the Witch unsuccessfully try to do to Aunt Letty?

   _____

   _____

   _____

3. What was Digory's plan to get rid of Jadis?

   _____

   _____

   _____

4. While waiting for the return of the Witch, what did Digory overhear Aunt Letty speak about?

   _____

   _____

   _____

5. How did "the Queen of Queens and the Terror of Charn" return to Digory's home?

_____

_____

_____

_____

6. What followed close behind Jadis?

_____

_____

_____

_____

7. As Digory attempted to get close to Jadis, who actually reached her first?

_____

_____

_____

THE MAGICIAN'S NEPHEW
Chapter 8—"The Fight at the Lamp-Post"

1. What did the people call Jadis to make fun of her?

   _____

   _____

   _____

2. What did the Witch use to hit the chief policeman?

   _____

   _____

   _____

3. What did Digory get hold of before shouting to Polly to get the yellow ring?

   _____

   _____

   _____

4. Who did Polly and Digory end up bringing into the Wood?

   _____

   _____

   _____

5. Why was the horse, in a way, responsible for them leaving the Woods?

   _____

   _____

   _____

   _____

6. What did the Witch call the place where they ended up?

_____

_____

7. What did the Cabby suggest that they do?

_____

_____

8. What then did Uncle Andrew try to do?

_____

_____

_____

_____

9. What was the first thing sung into existence?

_____

_____

10. Why did the Witch hate the singing?

_____

_____

_____

11. What was responsible for the singing?

_____

_____

_____

THE MAGICIAN'S NEPHEW
Chapter 9—"The Founding of Narnia"

1. As trees were popping up, what did the Witch stop Uncle Andrew from doing?

2. What do we find out about the Witch's activities back in London?

3. What did Jadis do before shrieking and running away?

4. What did Uncle Andrew wish to do to the Lion?

5. What had begun to grow that made Uncle Andrew think he could become wealthy by bringing scraps of iron to the land to bury?

6. What did Uncle Andrew call the land which made Digory want to go seek out the Lion?

_____

_____

_____

7. What happened to the animals that the Lion touched with his nose?

_____

_____

_____

8. List the commands which the Lion gave to Narnia.

_____

_____

_____

_____

_____

_____

_____

_____

THE MAGICIAN'S NEPHEW
Chapter 10—"The First Joke and Other Matters"

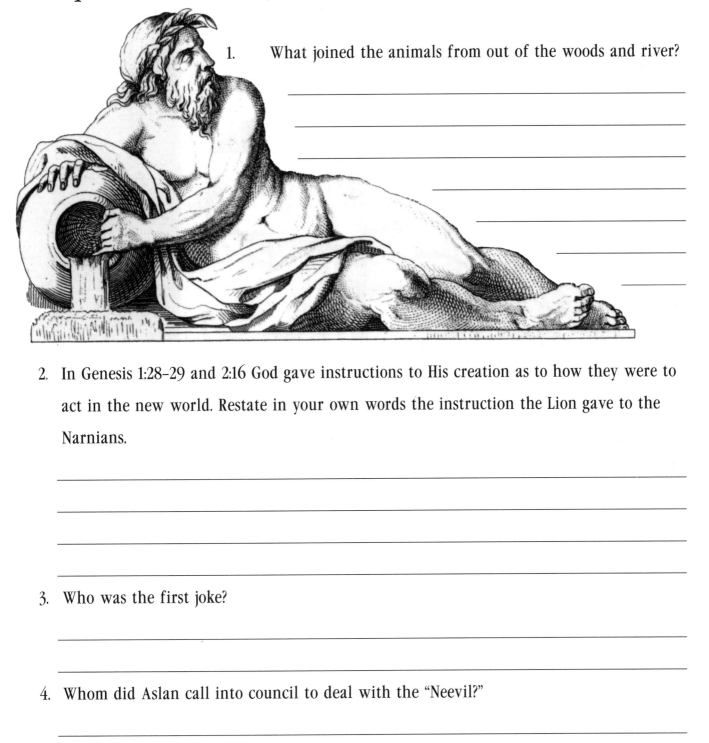

1. What joined the animals from out of the woods and river?

    _____

    _____

    _____

    _____

    _____

    _____

2. In Genesis 1:28-29 and 2:16 God gave instructions to His creation as to how they were to act in the new world. Restate in your own words the instruction the Lion gave to the Narnians.

    _____

    _____

    _____

    _____

3. Who was the first joke?

    _____

    _____

4. Whom did Aslan call into council to deal with the "Neevil?"

    _____

    _____

    _____

5. What white stuff did Strawberry want when he gave a ride to Digory and Polly?

_____

_____

6. Why did the First Joke scare Uncle Andrew?

_____

_____

_____

_____

7. After chasing Uncle Andrew, what did the Bulldog ask Mr. Ketterley on behalf of his fellow animals?

_____

_____

_____

THE MAGICIAN'S NEPHEW
Project—Narnia and the Bible

There are many times in the Chronicles that Lewis' stories remind us of stories in the Bible. In the last portion of Chapter 10, Uncle Andrew's perspective of the events are explored. Read Romans 1:18-23 and write a paragraph about how Uncle Andrew illustrates what this passage is about.

THE MAGICIAN'S NEPHEW
Chapter 11—"Digory and His Uncle Are Both in Trouble"

1. What did Uncle Andrew do after trying to talk with the dog?

   _____

   _____

   _____

2. What fell from Uncle Andrew's pockets when the Elephant tried to stand him on his head?

   _____

   _____

   _____

3. What did the animals decide Uncle Andrew was, in the end?

   _____

   _____

4. What did Aslan prophesy about the Evil Digory had brought into Narnia?

   _____

   _____

   _____

   _____

5. What "job" did Aslan give to the Cabby and his wife?

_____

_____

_____

6. What command did Aslan give to the Cabby and his wife?

_____

_____

_____

_____

7. What did Aslan ask of Polly?

_____

_____

_____

THE MAGICIAN'S NEPHEW
Chapter 12—"Strawberry's Adventure"

1. What did Digory see when he pleaded for Aslan to help his Mother?

   _____

   _____

   _____

2. What did Aslan prophesy about the Witch?

   _____

   _____

   _____

3. What did Aslan give to Digory along with his command to fetch a seed for the protection of Narnia?

   _____

   _____

4. Where was the tree from which Digory was to fetch the apple Aslan required?

   _____

   _____

   _____

   _____

5. What did Strawberry feel he had done to deserve Aslan's favor in making him a winged horse?

   _____

   _____

   _____

6. What did Polly provide for dinner?

_____

_____

_____

7. What did the children repeat to each other before they went to sleep?

_____

_____

_____

_____

8. What startled them before they fell asleep?

_____

_____

_____

_____

THE MAGICIAN'S NEPHEW
Chapter 13—"An Unexpected Meeting"

1. Following a dip in the river, what was for breakfast?

_____

_____

_____

2. Describe the outside of the garden.

_____

_____

_____

_____

_____

3. What was written in silver letters upon the gold gates?

_____

_____

_____

_____

4. What did seeing the phoenix keep Digory from doing?

_____

_____

_____

_____

5. Who else was in the garden with Digory, what had that person done and how did it change their appearance?

_____

_____

_____

_____

6. What did this person offer to Digory, if he would but stop and listen?

_____

_____

_____

7. What was Digory told was the identity of the apple he holds?

_____

_____

_____

8. What "fatal mistake" was made when trying to tempt Digory to steal an apple for himself and/or his mother?

_____

_____

_____

9. What was the only thing which reassured Digory on the flight back to Narnia that he had done the right thing?

_____

_____

_____

THE MAGICIAN'S NEPHEW
Chapter 13—The Toffee Tree

Pick your favorite candy and then decide what kind of tree it would create, if planted in Narnia on that first day of creation. Then in the spaces provided below, draw your candy tree and write a brief description of it—it's appearance and the nature of it's fruit.

THE MAGICIAN'S NEPHEW
Chapter 14—"The Planting of the Tree"

1. With what words did Aslan congratulate Digory upon his return?

   _____

   _____

2. What was done with the apple?

   _____

   _____

   _____

3. What had the animals decided to name Uncle Andrew?

   _____

   _____

4. What gift did Aslan give to Uncle Andrew?

   _____

   _____

5. Where did the gold come from for the King and Queen's crowns?

   _____

   _____

   _____

6. Which lands were Frank and Helen made King and Queen over?

   _____

   _____

   _____

7. What had grown up during the coronation?

   _____

   _____

   _____

8. What was it about this new
    Shield of Narnia which would
    keep the Witch away and so
    protect Narnia from her?

    _____

    _____

    _____

    _____

    _____

    _____

9. What did Aslan allow Digory to do after explaining
    what would have happened to Digory if he had sto-
    len an apple for his mother?

    _____

    _____

    _____

    _____

    _____

    _____

THE MAGICIAN'S NEPHEW
Chapter 14—Project

The poem by the Gate of the Garden is a special kind of poem called a quatrain. Quatrains are poems with four lines that have several different rhyming patterns. The rhyming pattern for this poem is ABAB (lines one and three rhyme/lines two and four rhyme).

> Come in by the gold gates or not at all,
> Take of my fruit for others or forbear,
> For those who steal, or those who climb my wall
> Shall find their heart's desire and find despair.

Write another verse to the poem in the meter and style of this poem that conveys either what Aslan says will happen to the Witch now or one that says what could have happened to Digory's Mother. There is a blank for the number of words each line is allowed to have. Remember to follow the rhyming pattern ABAB.

____ ____ ____ ____ ____ ____ ____ ____ ____

____ ____ ____ ____ ____ ____ ____

____ ____ ____ ____ ____ ____ ____

____ ____ ____ ____ ____ ____

THE MAGICIAN'S NEPHEW
Chapter 15—"The End of This Story and the Beginning of all the Others"

1. Before sending them home, what did Aslan show the children?

   _____

   _____

   _____

2. What would the children ever after remember if they felt sad or afraid or angry?

   _____

   _____

3. How long had the children's trip to Narnia lasted in our world?

   _____

4. What did Polly do as Digory was going to visit his mother?

   _____

   _____

5. What happened when Digory fed the apple to his mother?

   _____

6. What was remarkable about the spot Digory and Polly buried the rings?

   _____

   _____

   _____

7. Where did Digory and his parents go to live after his father returned home from India?

_____

_____

_____

8. Who became the first king of Archenland?

_____

_____

9. What became of the tree that Digory planted in London from the Narnian apple core?

_____

_____

_____

THE LION, THE WITCH AND THE WARDROBE
Chapter 1—"Lucy Looks into a Wardrobe"

1. Why did the four Pevensie children go to stay at the Professor's country house?

   _____

   _____

   _____

2. What were the names of the four Pevensie children?

   _____

   _____

   _____

3. Why did the children decide to first explore the house?

   _____

   _____

4. What was in the room with the dead-blue bottle?

   _____

   _____

5. Why did Lucy leave the door open?

   _____

   _____

   _____

6. What did Lucy find in the back of the wardrobe?

   _____

   _____

   _____

7. Describe the creature Lucy met in the forest.

_____

_____

_____

_____

_____

_____

THE LION, THE WITCH AND THE WARDROBE
Chapter 2—"What Lucy Found There"

1. What did the Faun call a girl?

   _____

   _____

2. What was the name of the Faun?

   _____

   _____

3. What were the boundaries of Narnia?

   _____

   _____

4. What did the Faun call the land Lucy was from?

   _____

   _____

5. Where did the Faun invite Lucy to visit?

   _____

   _____

6. What reward did the Faun say was given to those who caught the milk-white stag?

   _____

   _____

   _____

7. Who was the Faun working for as a kidnapper?

   _____

   _____

   _____

8. What had the Faun's employer done to Narnia?

_____

_____

_____

_____

_____

_____

_____

9. What token did Lucy leave with the Faun?

_____

_____

_____

_____

THE LION, THE WITCH AND THE WARDROBE
Project—Wardrobe

To add to the fun and magic of reading this book, you make a wardrobe.
Take a refrigerator box, cut doors into it and paint it brown. Or if you are in a classroom setting, decorate the door into the classroom to look like the wardrobe using butcher paper. Then decorate the inside of the classroom to look like a forest that is locked under a spell, making it "always winter and never Christmas."

The oak wardrobe on the right stood in Lewis' home and was, according to his brother, the inspiration for this book.

THE LION, THE WITCH AND THE WARDROBE
Chapter 3—"Edmund and the Wardrobe"

1. Why didn't the other children believe that Lucy had been to another world?

   _____

   _____

   _____

2. What were the children playing the next time Lucy visited Narnia?

   _____

   _____

   _____

3. Why did Edmund follow Lucy into the wardrobe?

   _____

   _____

   _____

4. What was pulling the sledge Edmund met with?

   _____

   _____

   _____

5. Describe those who rode in the sledge.

   _____

   _____

   _____

   _____

   _____

   _____

   _____

THE LION, THE WITCH AND THE WARDROBE
Chapter 4—"Turkish Delight"

1. What color was the Queen's small bottle of magic liquid?

   _____

   _____

2. What did the magic liquid make?

   _____

   _____

3. What did Edmund want to eat?

   _____

   _____

4. What royal position did the Queen offer Edmund if he
   brought his brother and sisters to her house?

   _____

   _____

5. What did Lucy call the Queen?

   _____

   _____

   _____

6. Where was the Queen's house located?

   _____

   _____

   _____

   _____

THE LION, THE WITCH AND THE WARDROBE
Project—"Turkish Delight"

Supplies

3 envelopes of unflavored gelatin

1/2 cup cold water

1/2 cup hot water

2 and 1/2 cups granulated sugar

1/4 teaspoon lemon extract

2 cups pistachios
    (or other nuts, if you like)

1/2 cup confectioners sugar, sifted

Directions

Mix gelatin in the cold water. Set aside. In a saucepan, bring hot water to boil and pour in granulated sugar, stirring constantly. Lower heat.

After the sugar is dissolved, stir in the softened gelatin until completely dissolved. Cook at a simmer for 20 minutes. Remove from heat and let cool for approximately ten minutes. Stir in the lemon extract and nuts.

Rinse a 6" square pan with cold water. The pan should be wet but not have standing water. Pour the mixture into pan. Cover and allow to stand in a cool place overnight. When thickened, cut into squares, and roll in confectioners sugar until well coated. Store in a box with added powder.

THE LION, THE WITCH AND THE WARDROBE
Chapter 5—"Back on This Side of the Door"

1. What nasty thing did Edmund do to Lucy?

   _____

   _____

   _____

   _____

2. Why did Peter and Susan eventually consult with the Professor?

   _____

   _____

   _____

3. In what subject did the Professor feel the children's education was lacking?

   _____

   _____

   _____

4. What three possibilities did the Professor suggest to explain Lucy's story?

_____

_____

_____

_____

_____

5. What made Lucy story likely to be true according to Professor?

_____

_____

_____

_____

_____

6. Why did Mrs. Macready give people tours of the Professor's house?

_____

_____

_____

_____

7. Why did the children all go into the wardrobe together ?

_____

_____

_____

THE LION, THE WITCH AND THE WARDROBE
Chapter 6—"Into the Forest"

1. What did the children take with them from the house as they explored Narnia?

   _____

   _____

   _____

2. What did the children find when they arrived at Mr. Tumnus' cave?

   _____

   _____

   _____

   _____

   _____

3. Of what crime was Faun Tumnus accused?

   _____

   _____

   _____

   _____

   _____

4. What is the name of the Queen's captain of the secret police?

   _____

   _____

   _____

THE LION, THE WITCH AND THE WARDROBE
Chapter 7—"A Day with the Beavers"

1. What object did the Beaver present to prove he was a friend?

   _____

   _____

   _____

2. According to the Beaver, who was "on the move" and perhaps already landed?

   _____

   _____

   _____

3. Where did the Beaver take to children for dinner?

   _____

   _____

   _____

   _____

4. What was Mrs. Beaver busy doing when the children arrived?

   _____

   _____

   _____

   _____

THE LION, THE WITCH AND THE WARDROBE
Chapter 7, Page 2

5. What was served for dinner?

_____

_____

_____

_____

_____

6. Describe Mr. and Mrs. Beaver's home.

_____

_____

_____

_____

_____

_____

_____

_____

_____

THE LION, THE WITCH AND THE WARDROBE
Chapter 8—"What Happened after Dinner"

1. What happened to Mr. Tumnus?

   _____

   _____

   _____

2. Who was Aslan?

   _____

   _____

   _____

   _____

3. In the *Magician's Nephew* we learn where the White Witch really came from, but from whom did Mr. Beaver say the White Witch was descended ?

   _____

   _____

   _____

4. What would end the White Witch's reign and life, according to the old rhymes?

   _____

   _____

   _____

   _____

   _____

5. What about Edmund did Mr. Beaver notice that made him think that Edmund had been
   with the Queen?

   _____

   _____

   _____

6. What event made the beavers insist on leaving immediately for the Stone Table?

   _____

   _____

   _____

THE LION, THE WITCH AND THE WARDROBE
Chapter 9—"In the Witch's House"

1. When Edmund left the beavers, what article of clothing did he leave behind?

    _____

    _____

2. As Edmund walked through the snow, what did he decide was to be his first act as King of Narnia?

    _____

    _____

    _____

3. What was crouching just inside the gate of the Witch's castle?

    _____

    _____

4. Who did Edmund think the statue was?

    _____

    _____

    _____

5. What did Edmund do to the statue?

    _____

    _____

    _____

6. Who was the first creature to speak to Edmund?

    _____

    _____

    _____

THE LION, THE WITCH AND THE WARDROBE
Chapter 10—"The Spell Begins to Break"

1. What did Mrs. Beaver bring with them?

   _____

   _____

   _____

2. Where did they stop to sleep?

   _____

   _____

   _____

3. Who did they see the next morning?

   _____

   _____

   _____

4. Why was it important that this particular visitor was able to get into Narnia?

   _____

   _____

   _____

5. What presents did they each receive?

   All: _____

   Mrs Beaver: _____

   Mr. Beaver: _____

   Peter: _____

   Susan: _____

   Lucy: _____

THE LION, THE WITCH AND THE WARDROBE

Project—"Gifts from Father Christmas"

Draw a picture of each of the gifts which the children received. Then read Ephesians 6:10-17 and list any similarities between the gifts.

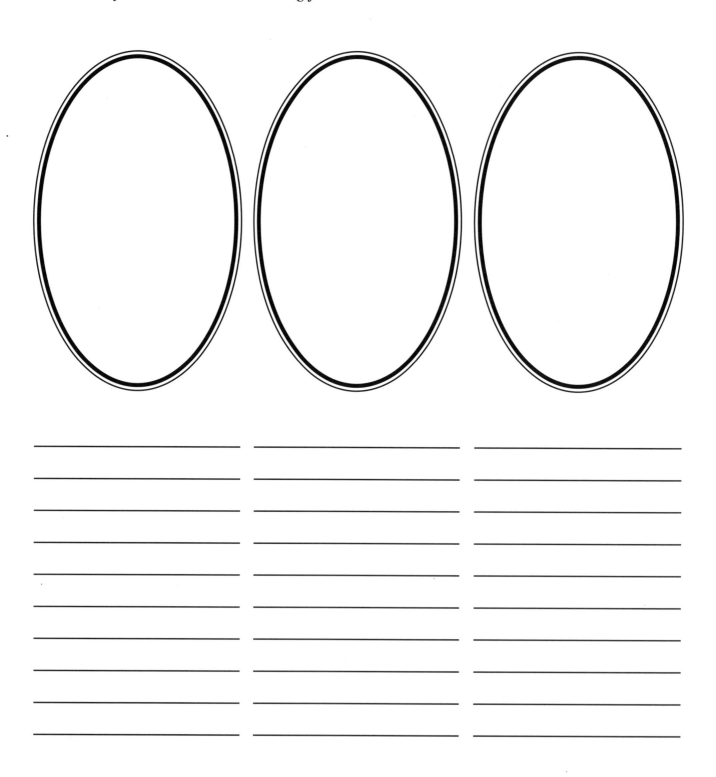

_____   _____   _____

_____   _____   _____

_____   _____   _____

_____   _____   _____

_____   _____   _____

_____   _____   _____

_____   _____   _____

_____   _____   _____

_____   _____   _____

THE LION, THE WITCH AND THE WARDROBE
Chapter 11—"Aslan is Nearer"

1. What did the Dwarf serve to Edmund to eat instead of Turkish Delight?

   _____

   _____

   _____

2. What kept the wolves from being able to track the Beavers and the children?

   _____

   _____

   _____

3. What did the Witch do to the group of animals who were sharing a Christmas meal given to them by Father Christmas?

   _____

   _____

   _____

   _____

4. What stopped the sledge's progress toward the Stone Table?

   _____

   _____

   _____

5. What did they do to Edmund when they couldn't journey anymore by sledge?

   _____

   _____

   _____

   _____

THE LION, THE WITCH AND THE WARDROBE
Chapter 12—"Peter's First Battle"

1. Describe the Stone Table.

    _____

    _____

    _____

    _____

2. Who stood around Aslan?

    _____

    _____

    _____

    _____

    _____

3. What did Aslan show Peter?

    _____

    _____

    _____

4. What alerted Peter to Susan being in danger?

    _____

    _____

5. What did Peter do that Aslan rewarded him with a knighthood?

    _____

    _____

    _____

6. What did Aslan command Peter to never forget to do?

    _____

    _____

THE LION, THE WITCH AND THE WARDROBE
Chapter 13—"Deep Magic from the Dawn of Time"

1. How did the Dwarf propose to keep the prophecy from being fulfilled?

_____

_____

_____

2. What did the Witch make the Dwarf and herself look like when the dagger was struck from her hand?

_____

_____

_____

_____

3. What requirement did Aslan place on the Witch if she wanted to meet with him?

_____

_____

_____

_____

4. Where was the Deep Magic engraved?

_____

_____

_____

_____

_____

_____

5. What would happen to Narnia if the Witch did not get blood for Edmund's wrong doing as the Deep Magic required?

_____

_____

_____

_____

6. What made the Witch pick up her skirts and fairly run for her life?

_____

_____

THE LION, THE WITCH AND THE WARDROBE
Project—Deep Magic

Using the chart below, translate the sentence found on the bottom of this page. Then create a model of the Stone Table or the fire-stones of the Secret Hill out of Sculpey® clay and inscribe it using the runes on this page. The Stone Table should be low—Susan and Lucy could kneel beside it without the top of the Table being over their heads. The fire-stones are only found in the British edition of this book where they replace the World Ash Tree (Yggdrasill) as one of the locations of the Deep Magic inscriptions. They would probably resemble Stonehenge.

A	B	C	D	E	F	G	H	I	J	K	L	M	N

O	P	Q	R	S	T	U	V	W	X	Y	Z

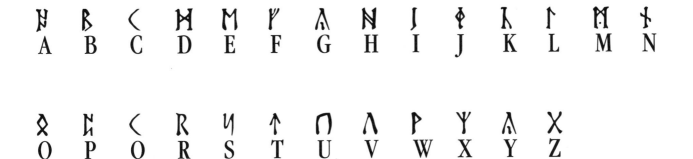

THE LION, THE WITCH AND THE WARDROBE
Chapter 14—"The Triumph of the Witch"

1. Where did the children and Aslan's faithful followers camp that night?

   _____

   _____

2. Who followed Aslan back out of the valley towards the Stone Table?

   _____

   _____

3. What did Aslan request because he was sad and lonely?

   _____

   _____

   _____

4. List those gathered with the Witch at the Stone Table.

   _____

   _____

   _____

5. What did an ogre do to Aslan once he was bound?

   _____

   _____

6. What pact had Aslan made with the Witch?

   _____

   _____

   _____

THE LION, THE WITCH AND THE WARDROBE
Chapter 15—"Deeper Magic from before the Dawn of Time"

1. What did the Witch set off to do as soon as Aslan was dead?

_____

_____

_____

2. What did Susan and Lucy remove from Aslan?

_____

_____

_____

3. Who removed the cords that bound Aslan's dead body?

_____

_____

_____

4. What time did the Stone Table crack?

_____

_____

5. What did Aslan do to prove to doubting Susan that he was not a ghost?

_____

_____

_____

6. What was the incantation from before Time began which worked the Deeper Magic?

_____

_____

_____

_____

7. What did Aslan do after his romp with the children?

_____

_____

_____

_____

8. To where did Aslan take the girls?

_____

_____

_____

9. How did they get inside the castle?

_____

_____

_____

THE LION, THE WITCH AND THE WARDROBE
Chapter 16—"What Happened about the Statues"

1. What did the effect of Aslan's breath on the statues look like?

_____

_____

_____

_____

2. What creature did Susan worry about Aslan bringing back to life?

_____

_____

_____

3. Who was Lucy happy to find upstairs in the Witch's castle?

_____

_____

_____

4. How did Giant Rumblebuffin help?

_____

_____

_____

_____

5. What did Lucy offer to the giant after his work?

_____

_____

_____

_____

6. Who set about organizing everyone as they set off to war with the Witch, and who actually helped the most?

_____

_____

_____

_____

7. After restoring the statues in the Witch's castle and throughout Narnia, what did they find when they reached Peter and Edmund?

_____

_____

_____

_____

8. Who was engaged in battle with the Witch?

_____

_____

_____

THE LION, THE WITCH AND THE WARDROBE
The Poetry of Narnia

Wrong will be <u>right</u>, when Aslan comes in <u>sight</u>,
At the sound of his <u>roar</u>, sorrows will be no <u>more</u>,
When he bares his <u>teeth</u>, winter meets its <u>death</u>
And when he shakes his <u>mane</u>, we shall have spring <u>again</u>.

Each line of the poem Mr. Beaver recited to the children about the end of the Witch's winter is actually a couplet with the last words rhyming, as indicated by underlines. In the space provided below, write a poem of couplets like the one the beaver recited but make it about the *Death and Resurrection of Aslan* or *The Great Battle Against the White Witch.* To begin, it may be helpful to make a list of pairs of rhyming words that refer to the topic you pick to write about. Notice that though the couplets rhyme, each line does not need to rhyme with the others. There are more lines than you need to fill.

_____

_____

_____

_____

_____

_____

_____

_____

_____

_____

_____

_____

_____

_____

THE LION, THE WITCH AND THE WARDROBE
Chapter 17—"The Hunting of the White Stag"

1. Who was responsible for smashing the White Witch's wand?

   _____

   _____

2. Why did Lucy get cross with Aslan?

   _____

   _____

   _____

3. What did Aslan do to Edmund on the battlefield?

   _____

   _____

   _____

4. Where did the high tea come from that they ate that evening on the grass?

   _____

   _____

   _____

5. Where did they reach the following day around tea-time?

   _____

   _____

   _____

6. Describe the Great Hall.

   _____

   _____

   _____

7. What "blessing" did Aslan offer at the children's coronation?

_____

_____

_____

_____

8. Who sang in honor of the new Kings and Queens?

_____

_____

_____

9. After Aslan slipped away during the great feast that night at Cair Paravel, how did Mr. Beaver describe the Great Lion?

_____

_____

_____

10. List a few of the deeds that marked the beginning of the Pevensie's long and happy reign as Kings and Queens of the Golden Age of Narnia.

_____

_____

_____

_____

_____

_____

11. What appeared that led to the rediscovery of the "tree of iron?"

_____

_____

12. When did the children tumble back into our world?

_____

_____

_____

13. Why did the children feel that they had to tell the Professor about Narnia?

_____

_____

_____

THE LION, THE WITCH AND THE WARDROBE
Project—Heraldry

During the Middle Ages, knights used a coat of arms to identify themselves. In a society where few people could read and write, pictures were very important. A coat of arms was like a label for instant identification—you wanted to know instantly who was coming toward you, so you could know which side he was on.

Shields are generally "read" starting at the upper left, going across and then down. A coat of arms can have several parts. The main part is a shield, which can have a crest above it, a motto, and animals supporting the shield. Traditional heraldry used only the following colors and metals (except for an object that was "proper," which means in its natural colors. A "bear proper" would be brown and a "tree proper" would be green with a brown trunk.)

Colors:

gold: generosity
silver or white: sincerity, peace
purple: justice, sovereignty, regal
red: warrior, martyr, military strength
blue: strength, loyalty
green: hope, loyalty in love
black: constancy, grief
orange: worthwhile ambition
maroon: victorious, patient in battle

The basic rule is "metal on color, or color on metal." This means that the background or field can be either a metal (silver or gold) or a color. The main object or objects should be a color if the field is a metal, or it should be a metal if the field is a color. Animals were shown in certain traditional postures, which were not meant to be realistic pictures of the animals (*Rampant:* standing on hind legs; *Rampant guardant:* standing on hind legs, face turned toward viewer; *Passant:* walking; *Couchant:* lying down; *Sejant:* sitting). They were not drawn to look three dimensional, but were shown as if they were flat. The pictures were to represent the animal as a symbol. Generally the animals chosen were fierce, and they were often shown in postures of combat. Often animals were combined to show characteristics believed to be found in more than one animal.

A common design on a shield was a pun on the family (last) name. The coat of arms for "Wheatley" might have sheaves of wheat on the shield. The cross on a coat of arms often meant that the original bearer had been on the Crusades.

Pick one of the Pevensies and, using the shield on the next page, design a coat of arms based on the titles they were known by during their reign in Narnia.

HIGH KING PETER THE MAGNIFICENT

QUEEN SUSAN THE GENTLE

KING EDMUND THE JUST

QUEEN LUCY THE VALIANT

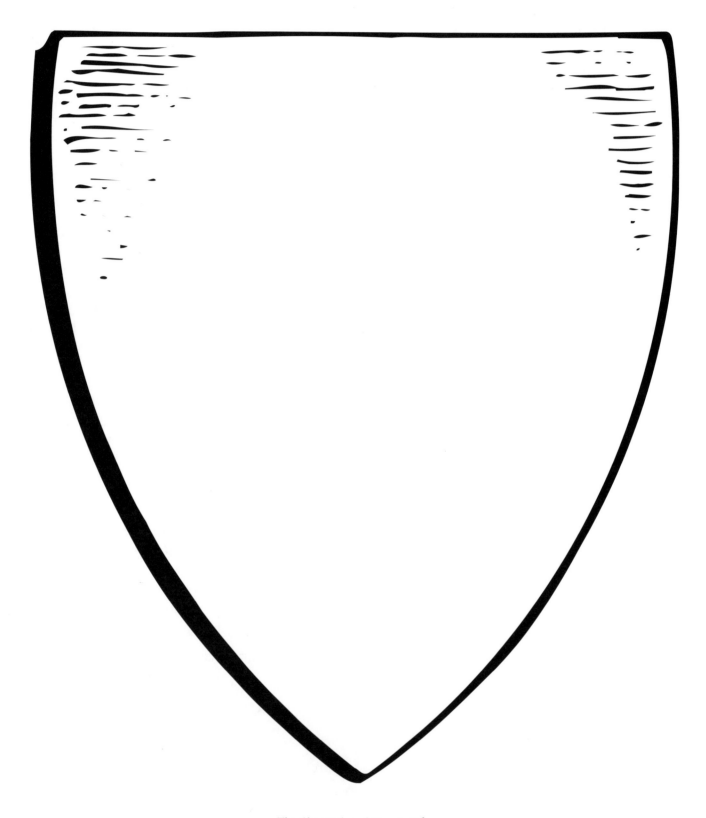

THE LION, THE WITCH AND THE WARDROBE
After The White Stag

The Pevensies returned to our world suddenly and without letting any of their subjects know where they went. Write an epilogue, a final chapter that describes what happened when the Kings and Queens failed to return home from hunting the White Stag.

_____

_____

_____

_____

_____

_____

_____

_____

_____

_____

_____

_____

_____

_____

_____

_____

_____

_____

_____

_____

_____

_____

THE HORSE AND HIS BOY
Chapter 1—"How Shasta Set Out on His Travels"

1. In Narnian history, when did this story take place?

   _____

   _____

   _____

2. What did Arsheesh do to earn a living?

   _____

   _____

   _____

3. Describe the Tarkaan who required hospitality from Arsheesh.

   _____

   _____

   _____

   _____

   _____

4. What did the Tarkaan want Arsheesh to sell to him?

   _____

   _____

5. What did Shasta learn about how he came to live with Arsheesh?

_____

_____

_____

_____

6. Why was Shasta comforted to find out that Arsheesh was not his father?

_____

_____

_____

_____

7. What did the Horse tell Shasta he should do instead of going with the Tarkaan?

_____

_____

_____

8. How was Shasta to hold on when riding the horse?

_____

_____

_____

9. What was the Horse's full name?

_____

_____

_____

THE HORSE AND HIS BOY
Chapter 2—"A Wayside Adventure"

1. Why did Bree say that it wasn't stealing to use the money Shasta found in the saddle bags?

   _____

   _____

   _____

2. What did Bree do following breakfast—which Shasta thought looked funny—and why was Bree so concerned about it?

   _____

   _____

   _____

   _____

   _____

3. Why did Bree not want to tell Shasta of the battles he had been in?

   _____

   _____

   _____

4. How long had they traveled before there was someone "shadowing" them?

   _____

   _____

   _____

5. When Bree and Shasta made for the shore to avoid the other horse and rider, what drove them back inland?

   _____

   _____

   _____

6. What drove the other horse and rider towards Shasta and Bree?

_____

_____

7. Bree was glad to be thrown near the other horse and rider because the Tarkaan could protect them. Why did Shasta find this situation personally unpleasant?

_____

_____

_____

_____

8. As they crossed an inlet, what did Shasta see behind him on the shore?

_____

_____

9. What do they discover about the Tarkaan's horse and the "Tarkaan?"

_____

_____

_____

_____

10. How are Bree and Hwin somewhat related?

_____

_____

_____

11. Instead of writing essays, what are Calormen children taught to do?

_____

_____

THE HORSE AND HIS BOY
Chapter 3—"At the Gates of Tashbaan"

1. Describe Ahoshta Tarkaan and tell what he had to do with the future of Aravis.

   _____

   _____

   _____

   _____

   _____

2. After learning of her parent's plans for her, what had stopped Aravis from committing suicide?

   _____

   _____

   _____

3. What did Aravis ask permission from her father to do after plotting with Hwin to escape to the North?

   _____

   _____

   _____

4. How did Aravis rid herself of the servant girl she had taken with her?

   _____

   _____

   _____

5. What did Aravis do in Azim Balda to gain more time?

_____

_____

_____

6. What did Aravis say would happen to her handmaiden for sleeping late?

_____

_____

_____

7. Where were the four travelers going to meet on the other side of Tashbaan?

_____

_____

_____

8. Whose plan for getting through Tashbaan did they end up using and what did it entail?

_____

_____

_____

9. What was the most painful part of preparing to enter the city which the horses had to endure?

_____

_____

_____

THE HORSE AND HIS BOY
Chapter 4—"Shasta Falls in with the Narnians"

1. Why was Aravis upset with how they were entering the city?

   _____

   _____

   _____

2. What does the soldier at the gate to the city accuse Shasta of doing?

   _____

   _____

   _____

3. What happened to Shasta when the Barbarian King and Narnian lords passed by the horses and the children?

   _____

   _____

   _____

   _____

   _____

4. Who did Queen Susan think Shasta was?

   _____

   _____

5. What was the name of the Faun who was among the Narnian courtiers?

   _____

   _____

THE HORSE AND HIS BOY
Chapter 4, Page 2

6. What does the Faun say that stops the Narnians from scolding Shasta?

_____

_____

7. How long had the Narnians been staying in Tashbaan?

_____

_____

8. What was the reason the Narnians were visiting Tashbaan?

_____

_____

9. What happened that inspired Sallowpad the Raven to quote the proverb: "See the bear in his own den before you judge of his conditions."

_____

_____

_____

_____

THE HORSE AND HIS BOY
Project—Tashbaan

Draw a picture of a city street in Tashbaan.

THE HORSE AND HIS BOY
Chapter 5—"Prince Corin"

1. Why did King Edmund declare that they were in danger?

   _____

   _____

   _____

2. What did the Raven speak of which captured Shasta's attention?

   _____

   _____

   _____

3. What had occurred the day before Calormen ambassadors came to Cair Paravel?

   _____

   _____

   _____

4. What did Mr. Tumnus suggest that they do so they could return to the Splendour Hyaline and fill it with supplies?

   _____

   _____

   _____

5. What did Shasta have for dinner?

   _____

   _____

   _____

   _____

6. What did the Faun speak of to comfort Shasta's "sunstroke?"

_____

_____

_____

_____

_____

7. What woke Shasta from sleep after dinner?

_____

_____

8. What was the boy's name who came through the window?

_____

_____

9. Why had the boy become separated from the Narnians?

_____

_____

10. What did the boy tell Shasta to do when he got to Archenland?

_____

_____

_____

_____

THE HORSE AND HIS BOY
Chapter 6—"Shasta Among the Tombs"

1. Describe the Tombs that Shasta found outside the city on the edge of the desert.

   _____

   _____

   _____

   _____

   _____

2. What made the harsh, piercing cries that Shasta heard?

   _____

   _____

3. What did the big, shaggy headed beast do to scare away the wild beasts and then what did it appear to turn out to be?

   _____

   _____

   _____

4. Why did Shasta get scratched?

   _____

   _____

5. What did Shasta do following his "raiding" breakfast?

   _____

   _____

   _____

6. Why did Shasta hurry back to the Tombs?

_____

_____

_____

7. What happened at the end of the day which was both wonderful and horrible at the same time?

_____

_____

_____

THE HORSE AND HIS BOY
Chapter 7—"Aravis in Tashbaan"

1. What fatal mistake did Aravis make after Shasta was taken by the Narnians?

_____

_____

_____

2. How did Aravis know Tarkheena Lasaraleen?

_____

_____

_____

3. Why did Lasaraleen want to open the curtains of her litter after Aravis closed them?

_____

_____

_____

4. What did Aravis learn about her father from Lasaraleen?

_____

_____

_____

5. What did Lasaraleen think of the Narnians?

_____

_____

_____

_____

6. Describe what Lasaraleen was like as a person and explain why Aravis thought she was silly.

_____

_____

_____

_____

7. Describe the palaces of Ahosta the Grand Vizier.

_____

_____

_____

_____

8. Why was Aravis unable to escape out of the city that first night using Lasaraleen's plan?

_____

_____

9. What did Aravis tell Bree they would do if Shasta was not at the Tombs as they had arranged?

_____

_____

_____

10. As Aravis was trying to escape, who turned up unexpectedly that forced Lasaraleen and Aravis to hide behind a couch?

_____

_____

_____

_____

THE HORSE AND HIS BOY
Chapter 8—"In the House of the Tisroc"

1. Why did the Tisroc not give his son ships that morning to pursue the Narnians when Rabadash saw that the Splendour Hyaline was missing?

   _____

   _____

   _____

2. Why did Rabadash repeatedly kick the Grand Vizier?

   _____

   _____

   _____

3. Why did the Grand Vizier suggest that it is not wise to attack Narnia?

   _____

   _____

   _____

4. Why did the Tisroc not want attack Narnia?

   _____

   _____

   _____

5. What did Prince Rabadash offer to the Tisroc that made him "the best of sons?"

   _____

   _____

   _____

6. Why was the capture of Anvard in Archenland a crucial part of Rabadash's long-term plans for Narnia?

_____

_____

_____

_____

_____

7. Why did Rabadash think High King Peter would not demand Queen Susan back from the Calormen?

_____

_____

_____

8. What did the Grand Vizier present as the differences between Narnian and Calormen poetry?

_____

_____

_____

9. What did the Tisroc confide to the Grand Vizier concerning his thoughts about the advantages of Rabadash failing in his expedition?

_____

_____

_____

_____

THE HORSE AND HIS BOY
Project—The Tisroc (May He Live Forever) Game

A storytelling game for 3 to 6 players.

Contents

One set of Tisroc cards

One set of Modifier cards

One set of Noun cards
> (There are blank cards in each set for the student to add words and phrases from *The Horse and His Boy* and also from our world.)

Gameplay:

For each round, one player is the Tisroc. That player receives the Tisroc deck and shuffles the cards, placing the pile face down in front of him.

The remaining cards are shuffled in two separate piles (keep the modifiers and the nouns separate). Each player other than the Tisroc is dealt a hand of four cards—one modifier and three nouns.

Moving clockwise and beginning with the player on the Tisroc's left, each player will:

MANDATORY: Draw one card, from either the modifier pile or the noun pile.

OPTIONAL: Trade cards with other players (not the Tisroc). While offering a trade, a player may only reveal the kind of card(s) being offered, not the content of the card(s). (e.g. "I'm willing to trade a modifier card and a noun card." is acceptable. "I have 'the world's smartest' and 'supermodel' for trade" is not.) Trades do not need to be "even"—e.g., a player could give away two cards and get only one in return, or get three in return.

OPTIONAL: Announce that they have three great compliments to pay the Tisroc and thus end the round.

If no player has ended the round before one player accumulates 10 cards, the round will immediately end at that point.

When the round ends, all players prepare to pay the Tisroc great compliments. The Tisroc flips over the top card in the Tisroc deck and places it face up on the table. The player who ended the round (either by announcing three great compliments, or by having 10 cards in his hand) goes first.

That player reads the Tisroc card and then plays two cards from his hand, first a modifier and then a noun, reading them aloud. The entire process will sound something like, "You are more powerful than... the world's largest... elephant." At least if everything goes well. If not, it might sound more like, "You are more beautiful than... the world's kindest... bath tub."

Each player, moving clockwise, does the same thing. Once each player has paid one compliment to the Tisroc based on the current Tisroc card, the Tisroc chooses the best compliment. The player who paid that compliment wins one point.

This process is repeated two more times, with a new Tisroc card revealed before each set of compliments. (If a player does not have the right mix of modifier and noun cards, he obviously cannot pay a compliment. However, if he has at least one modifier and noun, he must pay a compliment—no matter how goofy.)

In a game, each player is the Tisroc one time. At the end of the game, the player with the most points wins.

Game concept and rules by Erik Arneson.

diamonds	elephant	owl	mountain
horse	monkey	bath tub	lobster
dictator	pearl	princess	donkey
garden	desert	fish	castle

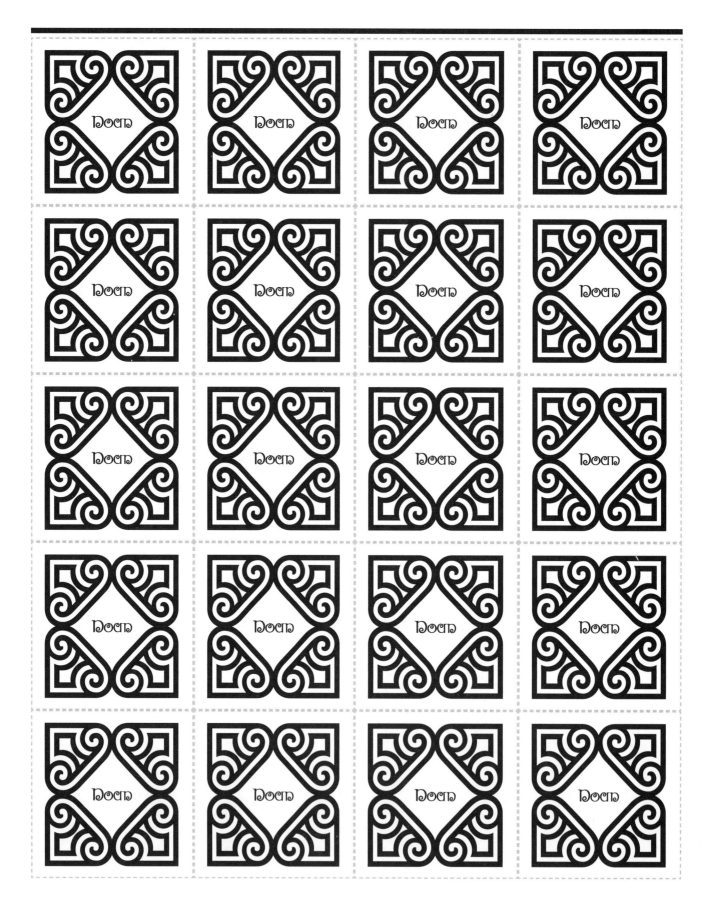

You are more beautiful than	You are more intelligent than	You are faster than	You are more powerful than
You are wiser than	You are in every way grander than	You are more regal than	You are more athletic than
You are wealthier than	You are kinder than	You are sweeter than	You are more humble than
You are greater than	You are more majestic than	You are more delightful than	You are more terrific than

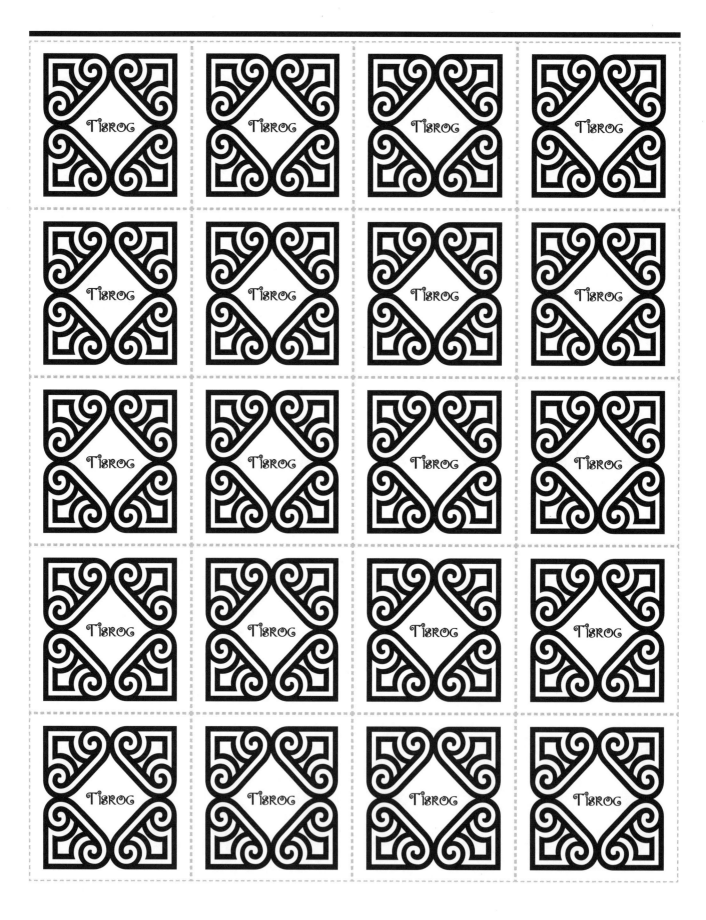

the world's largest	*the world's smallest*	*the world's wealthiest*	*the world's most beautiful*
the world's wisest	*the world's most intelligent*	*the world's fastest*	*the world's most powerful*
the world's grandest	*the world's most regal*	*the world's most sparkling*	*the world's kindest*
the world's sweetest	*the world's most humble*	*the world's best*	*the world's tallest*

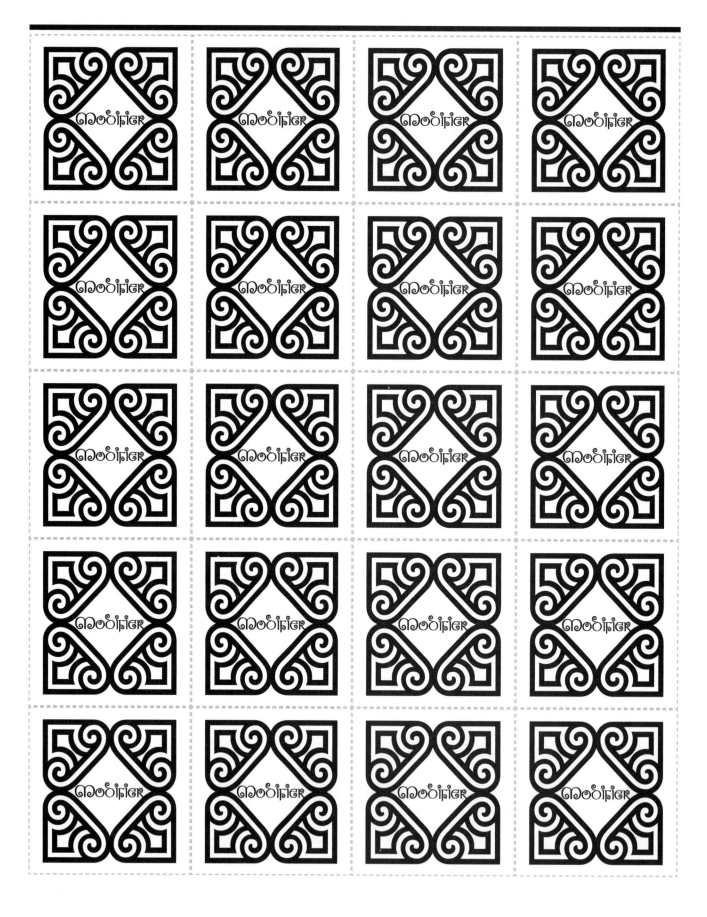

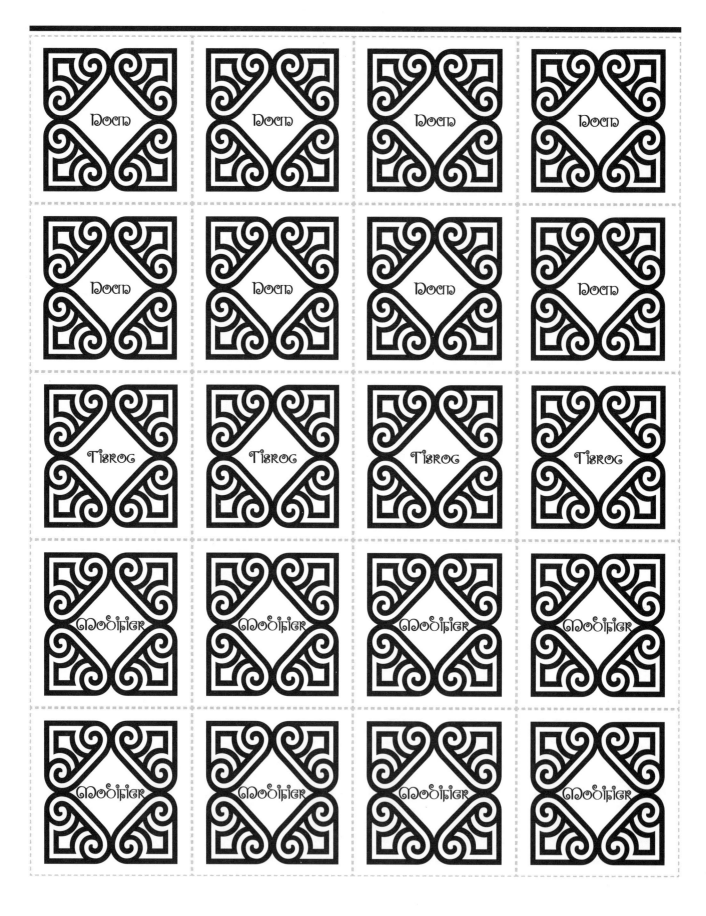

THE HORSE AND HIS BOY
Chapter 9—"Across the Desert"

1. What did Aravis threaten Lasaraleen with if she turned back and did not help Aravis to escape?

_____

_____

_____

2. What did Aravis say was lovely, as she hugged Lasaraleen goodbye?

_____

_____

3. What did Bree say that Rabadash had to do before he headed for Anvard, which would give the four runaways a head start?

_____

_____

_____

4. Why was Aravis able to take turns walking the following day, but Shasta was not?

_____

_____

5. What did they find about midday that was fifty yards long by thirty feet high, which gave them some relief?

_____

_____

_____

6. When did Shasta see the valley Sallowpad the Raven had spoken of?

_____

_____

_____

7. What big mistake did they make after refreshing themselves at the pool in the valley?

_____

_____

_____

8. What disadvantage did going across the desert towards the river valley have compared to going directly north by the oasis?

_____

_____

_____

_____

9. Who delayed them from setting off immediately for Anvard the next morning and why?

_____

_____

_____

_____

10. Who set the pace for their march the next day?

_____

_____

THE HORSE AND HIS BOY
Chapter 10—"The Hermit of the Southern March"

1. What landmark did they cross which signified their entrance into Archenland?

   _____

   _____

2. What did Shasta see behind them as they reached the first ridge?

   _____

   _____

3. Though the horses were galloping for Anvard as fast as they thought they could, what appeared unexpectedly which made them to go faster?

   _____

   _____

4. Describe the Hermit of the Southern March.

   _____

   _____

   _____

   _____

5. As Aravis was being attacked, what brave and foolish thing did Shasta do?

   _____

   _____

   _____

6. Describe the home of the Hermit.

_____

_____

_____

_____

_____

_____

_____

_____

_____

_____

_____

_____

7. By running straight, always straight, whom did the Hermit tell Shasta to go find?

_____

_____

8. How many scratches had the lion drawn across the back of Aravis?

_____

_____

_____

9. In all his one hundred and nine years, what had the Hermit never encountered?

_____

_____

_____

10. What gloomy plans had Bree made for his future?

_____

_____

_____

11. Though he thought he had lost everything, what did the Hermit say was the only thing that Bree lost when he ran to save his "own wretched skin?"

_____

_____

_____

_____

_____

_____

THE HORSE AND HIS BOY
Chapter 11—"The Unwelcomed Fellow Traveller"

1. Who did King Lune think Shasta was when he met him?

   _____

   _____

2. Why did Lord Darrin think Shasta had noble blood in him?

   _____

   _____

   _____

3. Why did Shasta's horse fall to the back of the procession?

   _____

   _____

   _____

4. What did Rabadash offer to his men if they were successful in quickly taking Anvard?

   _____

   _____

   _____

5. What happened while Shasta was up in the mountains feeling sorry for himself?

   _____

   _____

   _____

6. What did Shasta learn about all the lion attacks he experienced on his journey?

   _____

   _____

   _____

7. Why was Shasta not told the reason for Aravis being wounded?

_____

_____

8. What answer did the thing give to Shasta when the boy asked who the thing was?

_____

_____

9. What dreadful tales were told in Tashbaan about this one who spoke with Shasta?

_____

_____

_____

10. What did Shasta do when the brightness allowed him to finally see the one who he had

been talking with?

_____

_____

_____

THE HORSE AND HIS BOY
Chapter 12—"Shasta in Narnia"

1. What convinced Shasta that meeting Aslan was not a dream?

   _____

   _____

2. What was the first Narnian Shasta met?

   _____

   _____

3. What creature took the news of the invasion to Cair Paravel?

   _____

   _____

4. What did the dwarfs Duffle, Rogin and Bricklethumb serve Shasta for breakfast?

   _____

   _____

   _____

5. Who was the unlucky one who had to clean up their breakfast dishes?

   _____

   _____

6. Describe Narnia's flag.

   _____

   _____

   _____

7. List all the different kinds of members in King Edmund's army which Shasta saw.

   _____

   _____

   _____

8. What command of King Edmund's did Prince Corin not want to obey?

_____

_____

_____

9. Why was Queen Lucy unable to use her cordial to heal Thornbut?

_____

_____

_____

10. Who was responsible for getting Shasta involved in the battle?

_____

_____

11. What did Shasta wear into battle?

_____

_____

_____

THE HORSE AND HIS BOY
Chapter 13—"The Fight at Anvard"

1. Besides telling him about their secret escape from Tashbaan, what useful bit of help did Corin provide for Shasta?

    _____

    _____

    _____

2. Why was Queen Susan not riding off to battle with Edmund and Lucy?

    _____

    _____

    _____

3. What unique battle equipment had the giants carried with them?

    _____

    _____

    _____

4. After rolling off of his horse, how did Shasta injure himself in the battle?

    _____

    _____

    _____

5. How was the Hermit able to see the battle?

    _____

    _____

    _____

6. Instead of using ladders, how were the Calormen trying to gain entrance into the castle?

    _____

    _____

7. Who was Bree surprised to hear was among Rabadash's officers?

_____

_____

8. What brought down the men operating the ram?

_____

_____

9. Who led the charge out of Anvard?

_____

_____

_____

10. What did Rabadash yell just before he was unintentionally hung on a hook on the wall?

_____

_____

_____

THE HORSE AND HIS BOY
Project—The Narnian Banner

The Narnian flag is a rampant lion (an example is on the right) on a green field. During the Golden Age of Narnia, the lion is red. Draw the banner that the Hermit saw the wind catch as the reinforcements to Anvard came over the ridge. Or create the Narnian standard in the contemporary flag shape at the bottom of this page.

THE HORSE AND HIS BOY
Chapter 14—"How Bree Became a Wiser Horse"

1. Why was Bree reluctant to return immediately to Narnia?

    _____

    _____

    _____

2. What particular part of Aslan made Bree laugh at the thought of, then flee at the touch of?

    _____

    _____

3. What did Hwin say she would rather have done to her than be fed by anyone?

    _____

    _____

4. Read John 20:26-27. What does Aslan offer to Bree that is similar to Christ's interaction with Thomas?

    _____

    _____

    _____

5. Why did it turn out that Aslan tore the shoulder of Aravis?

    _____

    _____

    _____

6. Who did Aravis know his Royal Highness Prince Cor of Archenland as before his visit to the hermitage that day?

    _____

    _____

    _____

7. What had a centaur said at Cor's birth which so pleased King Lune and the Queen?

_____

_____

_____

8. Who kidnapped Prince Cor as a child?

_____

_____

9. Why did the children walk instead of ride to Anvard?

_____

_____

_____

_____

10. What was Bree's last act before they rounded the bend leading up to the castle?

_____

_____

_____

THE HORSE AND HIS BOY
Chapter 15—"Rabadash the Ridiculous"

1. What portion of their flight to the North had Cor not told his father which Aravis told to King Lune?

   _____

   _____

2. Who welcomed Aravis after she met King Lune, and helped her to settle in?

   _____

   _____

3. To what did Edmund refer when defending the possibility that Rabadash might improve for the better if his captors would show him mercy?

   _____

   _____

   _____

4. Who appeared among them as Rabadash shouted at the Narnian and Archenland kings?

   _____

   _____

5. What doom—or punishment—was inflicted on the Calormen prince?

   _____

   _____

   _____

6. Once Prince Rabadash's human form is restored, what must he do to avoid being changed back into an ass?

   _____

   _____

   _____

7. Instead of Rabadash the Peacemaker, what name was Rabadash found under in good history books of Calormen?

   _____

   _____

8. For what was King Olven famous?

   _____

   _____

   _____

9. Why couldn't King Lune orchestrate things to let Corin be king after his death, instead of Cor?

   _____

   _____

   _____

   _____

10. What was Corin Thunder-Fist's greatest exploit?

    _____

    _____

    _____

11. What famous heir did King Cor and Queen Aravis produce?

    _____

    _____

THE HORSE AND HIS BOY
Project—"Why Ram Was Great"

Add a chapter to the history of Archenland! Write a story telling what King Ram did that was so great.

_____

_____

_____

_____

_____

_____

_____

_____

_____

_____

_____

_____

_____

_____

_____

_____

_____

_____

_____

_____

_____

PRINCE CASPIAN: THE RETURN TO NARNIA
Chapter 1—"The Island"

1. How long had it been for the Pevensie children since they were in Narnia?

_____

_____

2. Who was the last to feel drawn into Narnia?

_____

_____

3. What were the children looking for when they discovered that they were on an island?

_____

_____

_____

4. Why did Edmund suggest they search the forest?

_____

_____

_____

5. What did they discover near the tree full of yellowish-golden apples?

_____

_____

_____

_____

_____

_____

PRINCE CASPIAN: THE RETURN TO NARNIA
Chapter 2—"The Ancient Treasure House"

1. What did they eat for supper that night in the ruinous castle?

   _____

   _____

2. What made Peter finally decide that they were truly back at Cair Paravel?

   _____

   _____

   _____

3. Who was responsible for originally planting the apple orchard?

   _____

   _____

4. What final test did Lucy offer up to confirm the identity of the castle?

   _____

   _____

   _____

   _____

5. Who wanted to wait until morning to clear away the ivy?

   _____

   _____

6. How did they find their way down the sixteen dark stairs?

   _____

   _____

   _____

7. What did they take with them back up the stairs?

_____

_____

_____

8. What was missing from their belongings they found and how was it lost?

_____

_____

_____

_____

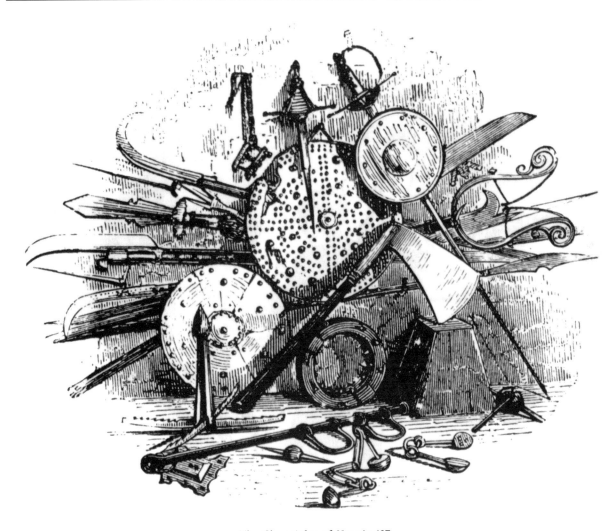

PRINCE CASPIAN: THE RETURN TO NARNIA
Chapter 3—"The Dwarf"

1. How does Edmund explain how broken down Cair Paravel has gotten in one year?

2. What did the children find floating towards them around the point of the mainland?

3. What did Susan do to stop the execution?

4. What do stories of ghosts have to do with this part of the story?

5. How did they carry the pavenders?

6. For whom did their guest to Cair Paravel serve as a messenger?

PRINCE CASPIAN: THE RETURN TO NARNIA
Chapter 4—"The Dwarf Tells of Prince Caspian"

1. What were the names of Prince Caspian's uncle and aunt?

   _____

   _____

   _____

2. Who taught Caspian about the Old Narnians—naiads, dryads, dwarves and fauns?

   _____

   _____

3. Decribe Doctor Cornelius and tell how he was to serve Caspian?

   _____

   _____

   _____

   _____

   _____

4. Who were Tarva and Alambil and what were their titles?

   _____

   _____

   _____

   _____

   _____

   _____

   _____

5. Why was the Great Tower a good meeting place?

_____

_____

_____

_____

6. What did Caspian learn about Doctor Cornelius up in the Great Tower?

_____

_____

_____

7. What did Cornelius call the reign of the Pevensie children?

_____

_____

_____

8. Why did the Telmarines invent stories of ghosts in the woods by the Eastern Ocean?

_____

_____

_____

_____

PRINCE CASPIAN: THE RETURN TO NARNIA
Chapter 5—"Caspian's Adventure in the Mountains"

1. Why did Caspian not study Navigation?

_____

_____

_____

2. Why did Caspian's life suddenly fall into danger after years of Doctor Cornelius' tutelage?

_____

_____

_____

3. How had Miraz removed all of those loyal to Caspian the Ninth following the death of Prince Caspian's mother?

_____

_____

_____

_____

_____

4. Before Caspian set off for the court of Archenland's King Nain, what two gifts did the Doctor give to him?

_____

_____

_____

5. What separated Caspian from his horse, Destrier?

_____

_____

6. Who did Caspian find had taken him in, once he regained consciousness?

_____

_____

_____

7. Who of the three was most desirous to kill Caspian?

_____

_____

PRINCE CASPIAN: THE RETURN TO NARNIA
Chapter 6—"The People That Lived in Hiding"

1. List some of the Old Narnians that Caspian visited that are mentioned.

   _____

   _____

   _____

   _____

2. What did squirrels think shows bad manners?

   _____

   _____

3. What did the Red Dwarfs give to Caspian?

   _____

   _____

   _____

4. Who did the Black Dwarfs wish to include in their company against the Telmarines?

   _____

   _____

   _____

5. For what did Glenstorm say that the time was ripe?

   _____

   _____

6. While Caspian and his new friends had supper, what did the Badger say that he wished that they had accomplished which would have made it "a good day's work?"

_____

_____

_____

7. Describe Dancing Lawn.

_____

_____

_____

_____

_____

_____

_____

_____

PRINCE CASPIAN: THE RETURN TO NARNIA
Chapter 7—"Old Narnia in Danger"

1. Why did the Bulgy Bears wish to delay the Council of War?

   _____

   _____

2. Whose sudden appearance interrupted the Council before it could even get underway?

   _____

   _____

3. What did Nikabrik want permission to do to the half-and-halfer?

   _____

   _____

   _____

4. Who betrayed Caspian to his Uncle Miraz?

   _____

   _____

5. To what defensible place did the Old Narnians decide to fall back?

   _____

   _____

6. What benefits did this magical place hold for Caspian's army?

   _____

   _____

   _____

   _____

7. Following a particularly bad day's battle with the army of Miraz, what did Caspian, Cornelius, Trufflehunter, Nikabrik and Trumpkin discuss doing?

_____

_____

_____

8. From where did the Doctor believe magical help would come?

_____

_____

_____

_____

9. Why did Cornelius tell Caspian to wait for sunrise to carry out their descision?

_____

_____

_____

_____

_____

PRINCE CASPIAN: THE RETURN TO NARNIA
Chapter 7—Aslan's How

Caspian saw on the smooth stones lining the tunnels in Aslan's How "strange characters and snaky patterns, and pictures in which the form of a Lion was repeated again and again." Considering what occurred many ages ago on that hill in The Lion, The Witch and the Wardrobe, *what might the images be? Add to the celtic "snaky patterns" below and draw what you picture the designs looked like.*

PRINCE CASPIAN: THE RETURN TO NARNIA
Chapter 8—"How They Left the Island"

1. What did the children discover about the way they were drawn back into Narnia?

    _____

    _____

    _____

2. How was Trumpkin caught by one of Miraz's men?

    _____

    _____

    _____

3. Why did the Dwarf decide he must return to Caspian and tell him that no help had come?

    _____

    _____

    _____

4. After they all were outfitted with fresh armour from Cair Paravel's treasure room, what did Edmund ask Trumpkin to do?

    _____

    _____

    _____

5. What was the outcome of Edmund and Trumpkin's broad-sword match, and what did Narnian air have to do with it?

    _____

    _____

    _____

    _____

6. What match did the children next suggest to the Dwarf, in order to prove their worth to Caspian's cause?

_____

_____

_____

7. What did Lucy do for Trumpkin after Susan beat him?

_____

_____

8. What did "D.L.F."—Edmund's nickname for Trumpkin—stand for?

_____

_____

_____

9. Describe the *Splendour Hyaline*, the children's ship from their time as kings and queens in Narnia.

_____

_____

_____

_____

_____

_____

PRINCE CASPIAN: THE RETURN TO NARNIA
Chapter 9—"What Lucy Saw"

1. Ater they rowed into Glasswater and had supper, they all fell asleep except Lucy. What did Lucy experience a little distance from their bivouac?

   _____

   _____

   _____

2. What were they attacked by about a half hour after they broke camp?

   _____

   _____

3. What horrible idea came into Lucy's head as they waited for the boys and the dwarf to finish dealing with their attacker?

   _____

   _____

   _____

   _____

4. What did Lucy see when they reached the Rush?

   _____

   _____

5. What decision did Peter make which upset Lucy?

   _____

   _____

   _____

   _____

Prince Caspian: The Return to Narnia
Project—Constellations

The constellations in Narnia have names just like they do in our world. Each is named for something that it looks like—even if the resemblance is very remote. Often the stars form the basic skeleton. Some of the Narnian constellations are the Ship, the Hammer and the Leopard. Draw a diagram of a Narnian constellation then a picture around it that illustrates it. Larger stars are shown as larger circles.

PRINCE CASPIAN: THE RETURN TO NARNIA
Chapter 10—"The Return of the Lion"

1. What happened that made them change their course of action and follow Lucy's direction up the gorge?

2. What did they have for supper once they had worked their way back up the gorge?

3. What were involved in a "country dance" when Lucy awoke that night?

4. Whom did Lucy find once she had made her way through the dancers?

5. Why did Lucy think that the one she met had grown larger than when she saw him before?

6. What strengthened Lucy after she learned of her responsibilty for the time lost that day?

_____

_____

_____

7. How did each of the other Pevensie children respond to Lucy waking them?

_____

_____

_____

_____

_____

_____

PRINCE CASPIAN: THE RETURN TO NARNIA
Chapter 11—"The Lion Roars"

1. There is a small argument about following Aslan, and though the D.L.F. thought it was all "bilge and beanstalks," who did he say he would follow should they split up?

   _____

   _____

   _____

2. Besides biting her lip, what kept Lucy from saying nasty things to Susan?

   _____

   _____

   _____

3. When did Edmund finally see Aslan?

   _____

   _____

   _____

4. What did Aslan tell Susan was the thing which kept her from seeing him earlier?

   _____

   _____

   _____

5. What did Aslan do to Trumpkin?

   _____

   _____

   _____

   _____

6. What did Aslan do after sending Trumpkin and the boys into the How?

_____

_____

_____

7. Who joined the trees in the dance around Aslan?

_____

_____

_____

_____

_____

_____

8. What grew madly during the Romp?

_____

_____

_____

PRINCE CASPIAN: THE RETURN TO NARNIA
Chapter 12—"Sorcery and Sudden Vengeance"

1. Why had the Horn *not* been blown immediately at sunrise?

2. What was Nikabrik's evaluation of the Horn's performance?

3. Who did Nikabrik wish to call on for aid since Aslan and the Pevensies had not arrived?

4. Instead of Aslan coming back to life after the White Witch killed him, what did Nikabrik think really happened?

5. Nikabrik said that the White Witch was a friend to dwarfs but not always so kind to animals. For what talking animals' extinction did Nikabrik credit the Queen?

6. What statement did the old woman make about a witch dying?

_____

_____

_____

7. Caspian identified the Black Dwarf's friends as what?

_____

_____

_____

8. What was the outcome of the conflict between those in the How's inner chamber?

_____

_____

_____

_____

PRINCE CASPIAN: THE RETURN TO NARNIA
Chapter 13—"The High King in Command"

1. What idea did Peter put forth as the next plan of action until Aslan would act?

   _____

   _____

2. What did Peter say would fill the day if they followed his plan?

   _____

   _____

   _____

3. What was the date Peter sent Edmund, Wimbleweather and Glenstorm to meet with Miraz?

   _____

   _____

4. What did the lords Glozelle and Sopespian plot?

   _____

   _____

   _____

5. Why had Miraz called for the two lords to join him in his tent?

   _____

   _____

   _____

6. As Glozelle and Sopespian lead Miraz on, what did Miraz say which upset Glozelle?

_____

_____

_____

7. What right did the eldest Bulgy Bear
   claim from the old times?

_____

_____

_____

8. What did Trumpkin say the Bear would
   do that would shame them all?

_____

_____

_____

_____

9. What did the High King tell Reepicheep was the reason that the Mouse should not serve
   opposite the Bear, Giant and Centaur?

_____

_____

_____

_____

PRINCE CASPIAN: THE RETURN TO NARNIA
Project—Chivalric Orders

Orders of Chivalry are primarily peculiar to Western European Christendom of the Middle Ages. Many were begun at that time, and among them are the Order of Malta, The Order of the Holy Sepulchre, the Order of the Golden Fleece, and others.

The origin of orders and decorations is found in the medieval organization of the Catholic monastic communities. The word "Order" (from the Latin *ordo*) referred at that time to an association of a limited circle of persons who took upon themselves certain obligations, and who subjected themselves to certain rules. At the time of the Crusades a number of Religious Orders of Chivalry were instituted, whose main objects were to fight for the Christian faith and to care for pilgrims and the sick.

In his letter to Miraz, the High King refers to the Order he belongs to and the one bestowed upn his brother. In the shields below, design an insignia for each order then fill in its name in the banners below.

PRINCE CASPIAN: THE RETURN TO NARNIA
Chapter 14—"How All Were Very Busy"

1. Who came to the combat, closing in behind the Old Narnians?

_____

_____

2. How did Trumpkin describe these beings whom Aslan woke?

_____

_____

3. Peter drew first blood by pricking Miraz in the arm-pit. What injury did Peter receive?

_____

_____

4. What did Glozelle and Sopespian do while Peter gallantly waited for Miraz to get up after tripping?

_____

_____

5. Who really killed Miraz?

_____

_____

6. What was the method the mice employed in battle with the Telmarines?

_____

_____

_____

7. What caused the Telmarines to flee down to the Great River?

    _____

    _____

8. What had happened to the Bridge at Beruna?

    _____

    _____

    _____

9. Besides the Bridge, what were other results of Aslan's holiday?

    _____

    _____

    _____

    _____

    _____

    _____

    _____

PRINCE CASPIAN: THE RETURN TO NARNIA
Chapter 15—"Aslan Makes a Door in the Air"

1. What did Caspian say which Aslan saw as proof of Caspian's being fit for office?

   _____

   _____

   _____

2. When Reepicheep appeared before Aslan, what was he missing?

   _____

   _____

3. What did Peepiceek tell Aslan they would do if Reepicheep was forced to continue on without a tail?

   _____

   _____

   _____

4. Following the knighting of Caspian, what was done with the Telmarines?

   _____

   _____

   _____

   _____

5. What did Bacchus, Silenus and the Maenads do for the Narnians once the Trees and Red Dwarfs had started a bonfire?

   _____

   _____

   _____

   _____

6. What did Aslan do thoughout the night once the feasting was over?

_____

_____

_____

7. What did Aslan cause to be set up fives days after the feast?

_____

_____

_____

8. Of what were the Telmars descendants?

_____

_____

_____

9. Among other things, what did Aslan tell Peter and Susan earlier that morning?

_____

_____

_____

10. What did Edmund accidentally leave in Narnia?

_____

_____

_____

THE VOYAGE OF THE DAWN TREADER
Chapter 1—"The Picture in the Bedroom"

1. What was the full name of the Pevensie's cousin?

   _____

   _____

2. Where were Peter and Susan while Edmund and Lucy were living with Uncle Harold and Aunt Alberta?

   _____

   _____

   _____

3. Describe the painting which was hung in the little back room upstairs where Lucy was staying.

   _____

   _____

   _____

   _____

   _____

   _____

4. When the children were swept into the sea, Lucy kept her head and did what?

   _____

   _____

5. Who dove in to help the children aboard?

   _____

   _____

   _____

6. What did the Pevensie's cousin do immediately after looking over the side of the ship for the picture frame?

_____

_____

_____

_____

7. What did Rynelf bring for the children to drink?

_____

_____

_____

8. What did Lucy resist doing when she saw Reepicheep?

_____

_____

9. Describe the room where Lucy was staying while on board Caspian's ship.

_____

_____

_____

_____

_____

_____

THE VOYAGE OF THE *DAWN TREADER*
Project—Paper Model of the Dawn Treader

Photocopy the artwork on this and the following page onto card stock (if you can enlarge the artwork, it works better). Color the boat according to the description in chapter one. Then cut out and assemble. The boat has been simplified in comparison to the one described in the book to help in construction.

Instructions

1. Cut out all the pieces.
2. Fold sides of boat toward each other. Fold the back panels toward the bow and the tail toward the stern, folding the tabs in along the bottom. Fold the tabs in along the bow.
3. Using glue or tape, adhere the tabs on the bow and the stern. The pointed portion of the bottom of the model will rest up inside the model. At this time adhere the tail and the head pieces together. Only glue the head—leave the neck to flare.
4. Fold over the tabs on the shields and attach to the inside of the boat.
5. Attach the flags and "crow's nests" to each other, then fold the tab at the base of the crows nest out. Fold the tabs of the sail and attach to the underside of the crow's nest—do not fold the tabs at the base of the rope ladder
7. Attach the tabs at the base of the rope ladder in the middle of the boat behind the shields. Then wrap the sail around the rope ladders, attaching the tabs along the inside of the boat, just behind the rope ladders.

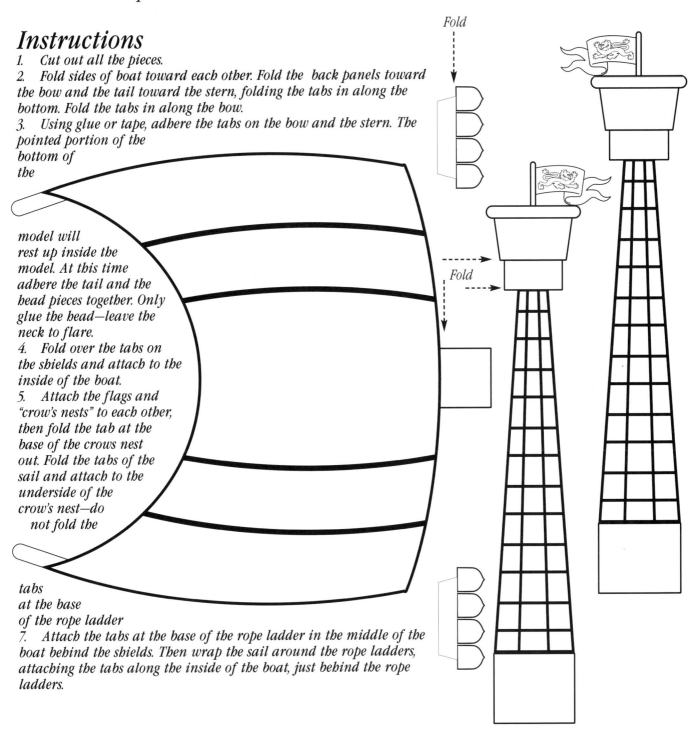

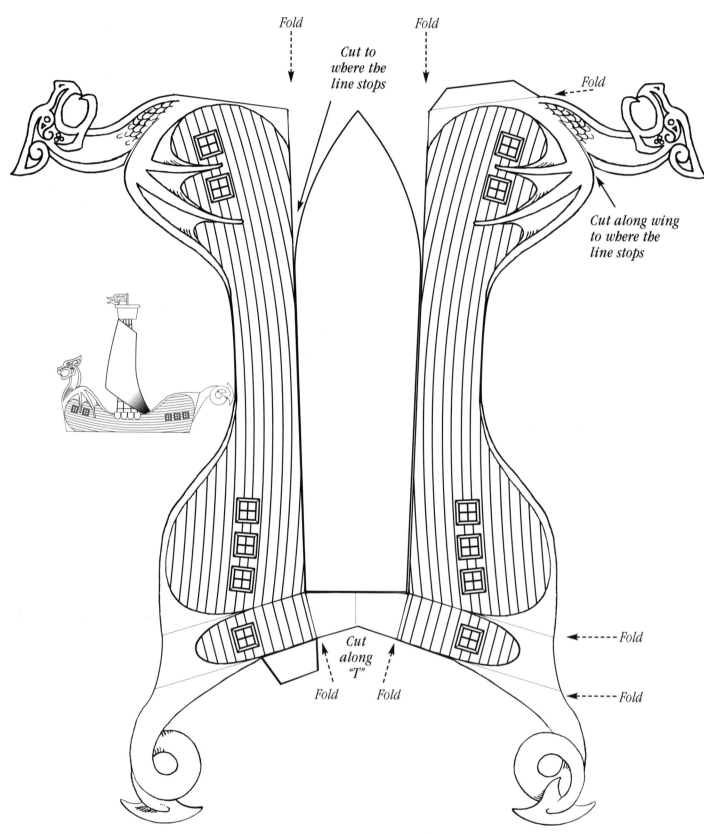

Fold

Fold

Cut to where the line stops

Fold

Cut along wing to where the line stops

Fold

Fold

Cut along "T"

Fold   *Fold*

THE VOYAGE OF THE DAWN TREADER
Chapter 2—"On Board the 'Dawn Treader'"

1. What was the name of the *Dawn Treader's* captain?

   _____

   _____

2. How many Narnian years had gone by since Edmund and Lucy had last seen Caspian?

   _____

   _____

3. What were the names of Caspian's father's friends for whom they sailed to find?

   _____

   _____

   _____

4. Where was it that Reepicheep hoped to reach on this voyage, and who or what put the idea into his head?

   _____

   _____

   _____

   _____

5. What was the sign Reepicheep was given to look for that would indicate that he had reached the utter East?

   _____

   _____

   _____

   _____

6. What did the Duke of Galma want King Caspian to do?

_____

_____

_____

7. How was Lucy able to cure Eustace of his seasickness?

_____

_____

_____

8. Where did the lookout stand in the forecastle?

_____

_____

_____

9. What did Eustace do to Reepicheep?

_____

_____

_____

_____

10. Why was Reepicheep's "correction" of Eustace such a new experience for the boy?

_____

_____

_____

THE VOYAGE OF THE DAWN TREADER
Chapter 3—"The Lone Islands"

1. Who wanted to visit Felimath?

   _____

   _____

2. How did Pug and his companions earn a living?

   _____

   _____

3. How much does Lord Bern pay for Caspian?

   _____

   _____

4. Why had Bern stayed on in the Lone Islands?

   _____

   _____

   _____

5. What was the name of the Governor of the Lone Islands?

   _____

6. What unwise act did Bern talk Caspian out of taking?

   _____

   _____

   _____

7. Following Lord Bern's advice, to whom did the *Dawn Treader* signal to assemble at
   Bernstead?

   _____

   _____

THE VOYAGE OF THE DAWN TREADER
Chapter 4—"What Caspian Did There"

1. Who initially led the cheers and bell-ringing upon Caspian's arrival to Narrowhaven?

_____

_____

_____

2. What did Caspian command to be done in the courtyard of the Governor's castle?

_____

_____

_____

3. For what was the Governor of the Lone Islands personally responsible to deliver to Narnia, which was one hundred and fifty years overdue?

_____

_____

_____

4. What did Caspian require of Gumpus, for which the failure to obey by Gumpus resulted in the end of the office of Governor of the Lone Islands?

_____

_____

_____

5. Who was Pug unable to sell?

_____

_____

6. What was done to the *Dawn Treader* to prepare her for the next part of their adventure?

_____

_____

_____

_____

_____

THE VOYAGE OF THE DAWN TREADER
Chapter 5—"The Storm and What Came of It"

1. How long was the Dawn Treader in drydock?

   _____

   _____

2. For the next few days, what did Lucy and Reepicheep spend a good deal of their time
   doing?

   _____

   _____

3. According to everyone (except Eustace), how long did the storm buffet the *Dawn
   Treader?*

   _____

   _____

   _____

4. What was lost during the storm?

   _____

   _____

   _____

   _____

5. Who kept Eustace from stealing water?

   _____

   _____

6. How many days passed after the storm until they anchored at the next island?

   _____

   _____

7. How many trips were required to empty the *Dawn Treader* of the whole ship's company using only the ship's boat?

   _____

   _____

8. Why did Eustace sneak off?

   _____

   _____

   _____

9. What new feeling gradually enveloped Eustace as he sat on the ridge?

   _____

   _____

10. What closed in around Eustace which made him lose his way when he tried to rejoin the others?

   _____

   _____

   _____

   _____

   _____

THE VOYAGE OF THE DAWN TREADER
Project—Reepichess

Chess is a game for two players, one with the "White" pieces and one with the "Black" pieces. At the beginning of the game, the pieces are set up as pictured to the right.

White always moves first, and then the players take turns moving. Only one piece may be moved at each turn. The Knight is the only piece that can jump over other pieces. All other pieces move only along unblocked lines. You may not move a piece to a square already occupied by one of your own pieces. But you can capture an enemy piece that stands on a square where one of your pieces can move. Simply remove the enemy piece from the board and put your own piece in its place.

 The King is the most important piece. When he is trapped, his whole army loses. The King can move one square in any direction. The King may never move into check—that is, onto a square attacked by an opponent's piece.

 The Queen is the most powerful piece. She can move any number of squares in any direction—horizontal, vertical, or diagonal—if her path is not blocked.

 The Bishop can move any number of squares diagonally if its path is not blocked.

 The Knight's move is special. It hops directly from its old square to its new square. The Knight can jump over other pieces between its old and new squares. Think of the Knight's move as an "L." It moves two squares horizontally or vertically and then makes a right-angle turn for one more square. The Knight always lands on a square opposite in color from its old square.

 The Rook is the next most powerful piece. The Rook can move any number of squares vertically or horizontally if its path is not blocked.

The Pawn moves straight ahead (never backward), but it captures diagonally. It moves one square at a time, but on its first move it has the option of moving forward one or two squares.

   If a Pawn advances all the way to the opposite end of the board, it is immediately "promoted" to another piece, usually a Queen. It may not remain a Pawn or become a King. Therefore, it is possible for each player to have more than one Queen or more than two Rooks, Bishops, or Knights on the board at the same time.

The main goal of chess is to checkmate your opponent's King. The King is not actually captured and removed from the board like other pieces. But if the King is attacked ("checked") and threatened with capture, it must get out of check immediately. If there is no way to get out of check, the position is a "checkmate," and the side that is checkmated loses.

You may not move into check. For example, moving into a direct line with your opponent's Rook, when there are no other pieces between the Rook and your King, is not a legal move. Otherwise, the Rook could "capture" the King, which is not allowed.

If you are in check, there are three ways of getting out:

1. Capturing the attacking piece;
2. Placing one of your own pieces between the attacker and your King (unless the attacker is a Knight);
3. Moving the King away from the attack.

If a checked player can do none of these, he is checkmated and loses the game. If a King is not in check, but that player can make no legal move, the position is called a stalemate and the game is scored as a draw, or tie.

Reepichess movements:

On the Dawn Treader, *Reepicheep always was getting himself into trouble by imagining glorious battles, then having his chess pieces act accordingly. In this game, Reepicheep will be given a fighting chance. Roll the dice on each players turn. Traditional rules of chess apply on a roll of 1-3, but on a roll of 4-6, Reepichess rules apply.*

 King—no change

 Queen—move like traditional knights

 Bishop—They become churches. They cannot move but they provide sanctuary to any piece adjacent to them diagonally—those pieces cannot be taken.

 Knight—Unlimited in any direction like a Queen under regular conditions

 Rook—They become strong towers. They cannot move but they protect any piece adjacent to them vertically or horizontally—those pieces cannot be taken.

 Pawn—moves 1 space in any direction (even backward) and it captures diagonally. It moves one square at a time, but on its first move it has the option of moving forward one or two squares.

THE VOYAGE OF THE DAWN TREADER
Chapter 6—"The Adventures of Eustace"

1. When did Edmund notice that Eustace was missing?

   _____

   _____

2. What crawled out of the cave in the valley Eustace had stumbled into?

   _____

   _____

3. Why did Eustace not recognize or know the name of the thing which he saw?

   _____

   _____

4. What event did Eustace witness that, when it was over, he "almost laughed out loud" with relief?

   _____

   _____

   _____

5. What drove Eustace into the cave?

   _____

   _____

6. What did Eustace find in the cave?

   _____

   _____

7. What did Eustace slip above his elbow?

   _____

8. Why did Reepicheep correct First Mate Rhince?

_____

_____

_____

_____

9. What woke Eustace?

_____

_____

_____

10. What did Eustace think lay beside him in the cave?

_____

_____

_____

11. What was strange about the tears Eustace shed while in the cave?

_____

_____

12. What caused Eustace to change form?

_____

_____

_____

13. Why did Eustace feel appallingly alone after leaving the cave?

_____

_____

_____

14. What did Eustace eat before leaving the valley?

_____

_____

_____

15. What was the only pleasant thing Eustace found in his new condition?

_____

_____

_____

16. What did Rhince think may have been the cause of the old dragon's death?

_____

_____

_____

17. Who was the first to speak to Eustace the next morning on the beach?

_____

_____

18. How did Lucy help Eustace feel better?

_____

_____

_____

THE VOYAGE OF THE DAWN TREADER
Chapter 7—"How the Adventure Ended"

1. Who was the previous owner of the golden bracelet on the dragon's arm?

_____

_____

_____

2. How did Eustace help his shipmates as a dragon?

_____

_____

_____

3. How many days was it after landing on the island before Eustace returned to his ship-mates in human form?

_____

_____

4. Recount how Eustace was undragoned.

_____

_____

_____

_____

_____

_____

_____

_____

_____

5. What happened to Lord Octesian's arm ring?

_____

_____

_____

_____

_____

THE VOYAGE OF THE *DAWN TREADER*
Project—Narnia and the Bible

There are many times in the Chronicles that we are reminded of a biblical truth. Read Ezekiel 36:26-27 and write a paragraph about how Eustace's time in the garden and the pool with Aslan illustrates what this passage is about. It is usually best to discuss this before having the student attempt it on his own.

_____

_____

_____

_____

_____

_____

_____

_____

_____

_____

_____

_____

_____

_____

THE VOYAGE OF THE DAWN TREADER
Chapter 8—"Two Narrow Escapes"

1. What did they take from Burnt Island?

   _____

   _____

   _____

2. Re-read the description of the sea serpent and draw a picture of it in color.

   [ ]

3. What was the brave, useless thing Eustace did?

   _____

   _____

   _____

   _____

4. What did the serpent break?

_____

_____

_____

5. What did Edmund sit on as they explored the next island?

_____

_____

6. How did Edmund test the depth of the pool they found on that next island?

_____

_____

7. Why did Edmund and Caspian begin to quarrel?

_____

_____

_____

_____

8. Whose sudden appearance ended the fight?

_____

_____

9. Why was Rhince glad to have located the third lord?

_____

_____

_____

THE VOYAGE OF THE *DAWN TREADER*
Project—Narnian Currency

Before naming it Deathwater island, Lucy finds "Lions" and "Trees," the everday Narnian coinage. On the blanks below, design your idea of Narnian money.

THE VOYAGE OF THE DAWN TREADER
Chapter 9—"The Island of Voices"

1. What was unique about the grounds of the island that they next visit?

   _____

   _____

   _____

2. What caused Lucy to become separated from the rest of the landing party?

   _____

   _____

   _____

3. What was the plan Lucy overheard the voices plot?

   _____

   _____

   _____

   _____

4. What was in the middle of the courtyard which Eustace was glad to see?

   _____

   _____

   _____

5. How many invisible enemies were there?

   _____

   _____

6. According to the voices, what kind of spell did the great magician set upon his servants?

_____

_____

_____

7. What was the task which the invisible creatures set before Lucy?

_____

_____

_____

_____

_____

THE VOYAGE OF THE DAWN TREADER
Chapter 10—"The Magician's Book"

1. What was Eustace's guess as to the possible form of their hopping hosts?

   _____

   _____

2. What is peculiar about how the invisible servers converse?

   _____

   _____

   _____

3. Describe what Lucy saw as she went up the stairs to find the Magic Book.

   _____

   _____

   _____

   _____

4. What was the most unpleasant aspect of how Lucy had to read the Book?

   _____

   _____

5. What spells did Lucy find in the Magic Book?

   _____

   _____

   _____

   _____

   _____

   _____

6. What kept Lucy from enacting the first spell which tempted her?

_____

_____

_____

7. How was Lucy betrayed by Marjorie Preston?

_____

_____

_____

_____

8. What was the story about that Lucy read which was called *A Spell for the Refreshment of Spirit?*

_____

_____

_____

9. After Lucy looked "almost as beautiful as the other Lucy" in the spell book, which creature did she see that she had made visible?

_____

_____

10. How was it possible that Lucy was able to make this greatest of all creatures visible?

_____

_____

_____

THE VOYAGE OF THE DAWN TREADER
Chapter 10, Page 3

11. What crime was Lucy accused of magically committing?

_____

_____

12. What promise was given to Lucy at the end of this chapter?

_____

_____

_____

THE VOYAGE OF THE DAWN TREADER
Chapter 11—"The Dufflepuds Made Happy"

1. Describe the person Aslan and Lucy met in the hallway.

   _____

   _____

   _____

   _____

   _____

   _____

2. Who was Aslan off to meet when he left Lucy?

   _____

   _____

   _____

   _____

3. What effect did invisibility have on Coriakin?

   _____

   _____

   _____

4. Coriakin served Lucy an omelette, cold lamb, green peas, strawberry ice, lemon-squash, and hot chocolate. What did he have for lunch?

   _____

   _____

   _____

5. What direct disobedience caused the Magician to cast the "uglifiying" spell?

   _____

   _____

6. What were some of the troubles Coriakin told Lucy he had with his charges?

_____

_____

_____

_____

7. Coriakin had many strange instruments in the room they used to look out onto the Duffers. Write definitions for the objects listed.

Astrolabe: _____

_____

Orrery: _____

_____

Chronoscope: _____

_____

Poesimeter: _____

_____

Choriambus: _____

_____

Theodolite: _____

_____

8. What brilliant idea did Reepicheep come up with that allowed the Monopods to take advantage of their unique feet?

    _____

    _____

    _____

    _____

9. Following dinner, what bit of useful and beautiful Magic did Coriakin perform?

    _____

    _____

    _____

    _____

10. What service did Coriakin perform for the *Dawn Treader* the following morning?

    _____

    _____

    _____

    _____

THE VOYAGE OF THE DAWN TREADER
Project—Coriakin's Map

In the box below or on another piece of paper, use the map in this book and the knowledge of the Eastern Sea you have gathered to create a copy of Coriakin's map. Cut out and glue down the magnifying glass on a part of your map then draw the detail of that spot like Coriakin's map showed when a magnifying glass was used on it..

THE VOYAGE OF THE DAWN TREADER
Chapter 12—"The Dark Island"

1. How long did they sail before they sighted the next island, and what did Lucy and
    Reepicheep spend most of their time doing as they sailed?

    _____

    _____

    _____

2. What reason did Reepicheep put forth as the reason they should sail on into the
    Darkness?

    _____

    _____

    _____

3. What does it mean that Rynelf was taking soundings?

    _____

    _____

    _____

    _____

4. What reason did the stranger who they brought aboard give for fleeing from this Dark
    Island?

    _____

    _____

5. As the sailors rowed and rowed, what did Lucy do in the face of being trapped forever
    in the Darkness?

    _____

    _____

    _____

6. What perched on the prow's dragon's head?

_____

_____

7. What was the name of the man they saved from the Dark Island?

_____

_____

8. What request did the stranger make of Caspian?

_____

_____

_____

_____

THE VOYAGE OF THE DAWN TREADER
Chapter 13—"The Three Sleepers"

1. Describe the place where the adventurers found the sumptuously spread dining table on the island some called World's End.

   _____

   _____

   _____

   _____

   _____

2. Who did they find sleeping at the table?

   _____

   _____

   _____

3. Describe the girl who came to them just before sunrise.

   _____

   _____

   _____

   _____

   _____

4. What caused the enchantment over the sleepers at the table?

   _____

   _____

   _____

   _____

5. Identify and describe the sacred relic kept in honor on the table.

_____

_____

_____

_____

6. Who chose to believe about the safety of the food on the table, and then drinks to the lady?

_____

_____

7. To what fairy tale did Caspian refer when seeking to discover how to make the sleepers awake?

_____

_____

8. How did the enchantment on the men at Aslan's Table differ from the one Caspian described?

_____

_____

_____

_____

_____

_____

_____

THE VOYAGE OF THE DAWN TREADER
Chapter 13—Knife of Stone

". . . [the knife] that the White Witch used when she killed Aslan at the Stone Table long ago . . . brought here to be kept in honour while the world lasts."

Supplies:

Black Granite Make It Stone!® spray paint

Acrylic Crystal Clear

Glue

Twine

Directions:

Trace the shape to the right, or one of your own, onto cardboard. Then trace twice the two portions of the hilt indicated by the brackets on cardboard. Cut out all five pieces. Glue the duplicate hilt pieces on top and bottom of the entire blade cut out. These will add depth and help hold the handle in place. Follow the directions on the spray can, painting both sides of the knife to look like stone. After the paint is dry, wrap the hand grip (between the extra top and bottom pieces) with the twine until it is the necessary thickness to fit well in your hand. Glue the end of the twine down then spray the entire knife with clear fixative.

THE VOYAGE OF THE DAWN TREADER
Chapter 14—"The Beginning of the End of the World"

1. When the girl's father appeared, what did he and his daughter do?

   _____

   _____

2. What came from the sun, and what did one of this company do to the Old Man?

   _____

   _____

   _____

3. How was the enchantment over the sleepers to be broken?

   _____

   _____

   _____

   _____

4. What did Ramandu do before he lived on the island called World's End?

   _____

   _____

5. What did the travellers learn about Coriakin?

   _____

   _____

   _____

6. What sailing misunderstanding—landsman's talk—did the Master Bowman voice about their return to Narnia?

_____

_____

_____

7. What did Caspian say he would give to every man who sailed with them beyond the Island of the Star?

_____

_____

_____

8. What did Ramandu give to Lord Rhoop?

_____

_____

9. What creatures did the sailor Pittencream develop a dislike for, which he carried with him until the end of his days?

_____

_____

10. What desire did Caspian voice just before they set sail the following day?

_____

_____

_____

THE VOYAGE OF THE DAWN TREADER
Chapter 15—"The Wonders of the Last Sea"

1. What were some of the changes once they left the Island of the Star?

   _____

   _____

   _____

2. Describe the Sea People.

   _____

   _____

   _____

3. What discovery did Reepicheep fall into?

   _____

   _____

   _____

4. What effect did the "Drinkable Light" have on those aboard
   the *Dawn Treader?*

   _____

   _____

   _____

5. What concern did the strong current put into their minds?

   _____

   _____

   _____

6. What difference did Eustace learn about Narnia versus our world?

   _____

   _____

THE VOYAGE OF THE DAWN TREADER
Chapter 16—"The Very End of the World"

1. What made the Silver Sea "silver?"

_____

_____

2. What did they learn about the current they were in which gave them comfort when contemplating the journey back to Ramandu's island?

_____

_____

_____

3. What did Caspian want to do that Edmund and the rest of the crew had to confront him on?

_____

_____

_____

4. What Greek hero did Edmund refer to as they all tried to talk the King out of his rash descision?

_____

_____

5. What did Aslan tell Caspian when he spoke to him in the King's cabin?

_____

_____

_____

_____

6. What stretched out before them when they ran aground, and what could they see beyond it?

_____

_____

_____

7. What happened to Reepicheep the Mouse?

_____

_____

_____

8. What did the children see between them and the foot of the sky once they had walked out of the water onto the grass?

_____

_____

9. What did the great Bridge Builder tell the children about the way into his country?

_____

_____

_____

10. How did Aslan comfort Lucy when she sobbed, "how can we live, never meeting you?"

_____

_____

_____

_____

11. What do we learn in the end about Ramandu's daughter?

_____

_____

_____

_____

_____

THE SILVER CHAIR
Chapter 1—"Behind the Gym"

1. Why was Jill Pole crying behind the gym?

   _____

   _____

2. Why did *They* decide Eustace Scrubb needed "attending" to?

   _____

   _____

   _____

3. What did Scrubb tell Jill he had done over the holidays?

   _____

   _____

4. Why did Scrubb decide against Jill's idea of drawing a circle and standing in it to recite spells?

   _____

   _____

5. What did Scrubb suggest they try which he had seen Ramandu do?

   _____

   _____

6. How did they get off of the school grounds, out of our world and into That Place?

   _____

   _____

7. What sound replaced that of Edith Jackle's voice being switched off like a radio?

_____

_____

8. What caused Jill to despise Scrubb when they reached the edge of the woods?

_____

_____

_____

9. What terrifying thing happened to Scrubb?

_____

_____

_____

10. What kind of creature rushed up next to Jill when Scrubb was gone?

_____

_____

THE SILVER CHAIR
Chapter 2—"Jill is Given a Task"

1. After the Lion left her, what caused Jill to cry?

   _____

   _____

2. When Jill eventually stopped crying, what drove her to get up and begin exploring the woods?

   _____

   _____

3. How did the Lion respond to Jill's question whether or not he ate girls?

   _____

   _____

4. Why did Jill think that the Lion had mistaken her for someone else?

   _____

   _____

5. What was Jill told was the only condition under which the children would have ever called for the help of Aslan?

   _____

   _____

6. What task did Aslan set before Jill?

   _____

   _____

7. List the four signs.

   1._____

   _____

   2._____

   _____

   3._____

   _____

   4._____

_____

8. Aslan urged her to "Remember the signs and believe the signs." Why did Aslan say it would be hard for her to follow the signs?

_____

_____

_____

_____

_____

9. What did Aslan say she should do so she would not forget the signs?

_____

_____

_____

10. How did Jill travel to Narnia?

_____

_____

_____

THE SILVER CHAIR
Project—Narnia and the Bible

Jill thought Aslan had mistaken her for someone else because it was she and Scrubb who had done the calling to enter Narnia. Read John 15:16, Romans 8:29–30, Ephesians 1:11–12 and Colossians 3:12–13 then write a paragraph about how Aslan's answer to Jill illustrates what these passages are about.

_____

_____

_____

_____

_____

_____

_____

_____

_____

_____

_____

_____

_____

_____

_____

_____

_____

THE SILVER CHAIR
Chapter 3—"The Sailing of the King"

1. Who was the only one to see Scrubb and Jill fly into Narnia?

   _____

   _____

2. What was the name of the King who sailed away soon after the children arrive?

   _____

   _____

3. Who was the hard-of-hearing Lord Regent?

   _____

   _____

4. What part of their task were the children told *not* to reveal to the Lord Regent?

   _____

   _____

5. Why did Scrubb and Jill not know that they were a Son of Adam and Daughter of Eve?

   _____

   _____

6. Describe the room the dryad took Jill to.

   _____

   _____

   _____

   _____

7. How did the children muff the first Sign?

_____

_____

_____

8. How did Scrubb account for the children arriving in Narnia only about a minute apart?

_____

_____

_____

_____

9. What was served for dinner in Cair Paravel's banner-decked great hall?

_____

_____

_____

10. What was the tale the blind bard told after their supper?

_____

_____

_____

THE SILVER CHAIR
Chapter 3, Project—Narnian Banner

Using your knowledge of Narnian history, design a banner for the Great Hall of Cair Paravel.

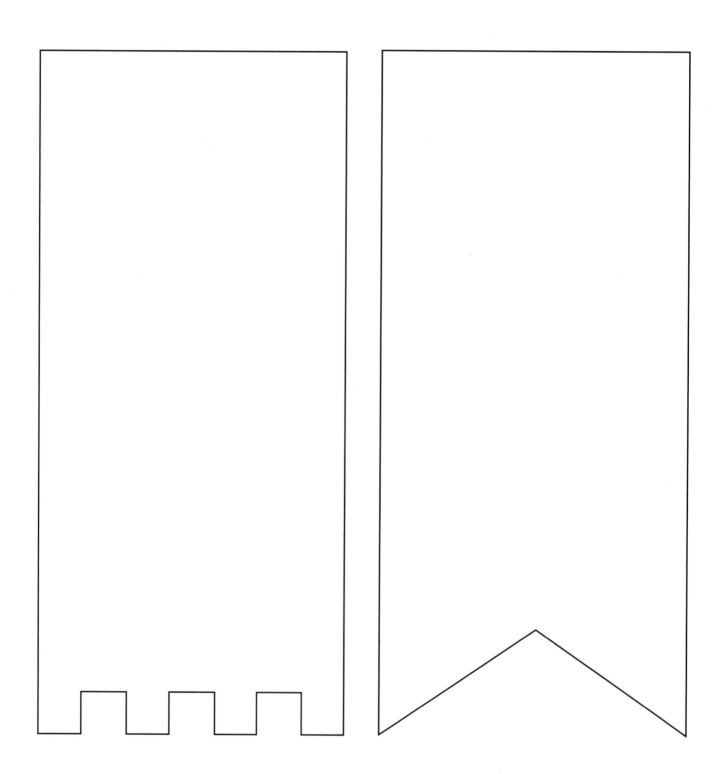

THE SILVER CHAIR
Chapter 4—"A Parliament of Owls"

1. What did Scrubb wish to make clear before the parliament began?

   _____

   _____

   _____

   _____

2. Why would Trumpkin prohibit the children from following the orders of Aslan?

   _____

   _____

   _____

   _____

   _____

3. Why did the owls think the King would want to sail on beyond the Lone Islands if he did not meet Aslan in Terebinthia?

   _____

   _____

   _____

   _____

4. Why did the owls meet in the dead of night if their intentions truly meant no mischief?

   _____

   _____

   _____

   _____

5. Describe what happened to Ramandu's Daughter—the mother of Rilian.

_____

_____

_____

_____

_____

_____

6. What did Lord Drinian see when he rode out with the Prince several weeks later?

_____

_____

_____

7. What did Caspian do when Drinian told him about witholding the information about the mysterious lady clad in green?

_____

_____

_____

8. What made the owls not want to help the children search for the Prince?

_____

_____

_____

9. Who did the owls propose as the best people to help the children into Ettinsmoor?

_____

_____

_____

THE SILVER CHAIR
Chapter 5—"Puddleglum"

1. Describe the appearance of Marsh-wiggles.

   _____

   _____

   _____

   _____

   _____

2. What were a few of the gloomy predictions Puddleglum offered the children when they officially met in the morning?

   _____

   _____

   _____

   _____

   _____

3. What had the other wiggles told Puddleglum in the past—for his own good—was wrong with him, which made him feel this adventure was such a good opportunity?

   _____

   _____

   _____

4. When had Scrubb learned archery?

   _____

   _____

5. What caused the children to have a bad night's sleep?

   _____

   _____

THE SILVER CHAIR
Chapter 5—Marsh-wiggle Illustration

C. S. Lewis based Puddleglum on his pessimistic gardener, Fred Paxford. Since Marsh-wiggles were created for The Silver Chair, *there haven't been many illustrative interpretations of the creatures. Re-read the passage from this chapter when the children first meet Puddleglum and draw him, trying to forget Pauline Baynes' illustrations for the moment.*

THE SILVER CHAIR
The Puddleglum and the Prince Game

"Marsh-Wiggles are people who like privacy." In this game, a player's first job is to find Puddleglum. Then the task becomes to locate Prince Rilian. A game of discovery for 2 to 4 players.

Components:

4 player tokens
47 Cards divided into 3 sets (see below)
36 Victory Point markers; pennies would work quite well (You could also use a nickel to represent 5 VPs, and a dime to represent 10 VPs.)

Set 1 includes 16 cards:
1 blank start square, worth no victory points
3 "Move an Existing Card—Cost 1 VP"
3 "Move Another Space"
4 "Play an Extra Card"
5 blank, worth 1 victory point each

Set 2 includes 20 cards:
1 Puddleglum, worth 4 victory points
2 "Move an Existing Card—Cost 1 VP"
3 "Play an Extra Card"
5 "Move Another Space"
9 blank, worth 1 victory point each

Set 3 includes 13 cards:
1 Prince, worth 7 victory points
3 "Move Another Space"
7 blank, worth 1 victory point each

Setup:

Place the start card on the table. The cards will form the game board, and this will be the bottom right corner of the board when it's complete (the total board size will be 7 cards x 7 cards), so place it with that fact in mind.

Shuffle each set of cards separately, and set them in piles face down where every player can reach them.

Turn over the top 3 cards from Set 1, one at a time, and place them next to the start square. When this step is finished, you will have a 2x2 square with the start square still at the bottom right corner. The start square will always be the bottom right corner of the board.

All players set their tokens on the start square. The first player to move is chosen randomly.

Gameplay:

On a turn, a player flips over the top card of the current set and then plays it to the board. (Once the cards from Set 1 are exhausted, players draw from Set 2. Once Set 2 is exhausted, they draw from Set 3. Once Set 3 is exhausted, they skip this part of the turn.)

The drawn card must be played adjacent to another card already on the board, subject to the following restrictions:

1. "Adjacent" means horizontally or vertically adjacent, not diagonally.
2. Cards from set 1 will be used to form a 4x4 square. They cannot extend outside of that square.
3. Cards from Set 2 will add 2 rows and columns to the board, so that it will be 6x6 when Set 2 is exhausted.
4. Cards from Set 3 will expand the board to 7x7.
5. The start card must always remain in the bottom right corner.

After playing a card, a player moves his token one space horizontally or vertically and then responds to the card landed on. Many cards are optional; that is, a player is not forced to take the action on the card.

Cards:

Move Another Space
The player may move one additional space, but only horizontally or vertically.

Play an Extra Card
The player may draw and play an extra card, subject to the normal restrictions.

Move an Existing Card (cost 1 VP)
The player may move a card already on the board to a new location. However, at the new location it must be adjacent to another card on the board. A moved card can only be played to an empty spot (swapping cards it not permitted). Additionally, all Set 1 cards must remain in the 4x4 square, and Set 2 cards must remain in the 6x6 square. It costs one victory point to move a card in this manner. If a player has no victory points, that player cannot move a card. A paid victory point is removed from the game.

Blank (worth 1 VP)
The first player to land on each of these cards wins one victory point. To help keep track, it is recommended that a VP marker (e.g., a penny) be placed on each of these cards as soon as they are played. When a player lands on the card, the VP marker is removed and that player keeps it.

Puddleglum
The first player to land on (find) Puddleglum wins 4 victory points.

Prince Rilian
The first player to land on (find) Prince Rilian wins 7 victory points. The game ends immediately when a player lands on Prince Rilian. (NOTE: It is possible, in rare cases, that Prince Rilian will be found before Puddleglum is found.)

Victory Points and the End of the Game

Players must take the VPs when they are available—this is not optional. At the end of the game, players total their victory points. The winner is the player with the most victory points. During the game, players should keep their victory points secret from each other so that no one can be sure (without concentrating very hard, anyway) of how many VPs their opponents have.

Game concept and rules by Erik Arneson.

Start	Move an Existing Card	Move an Existing Card	Move an Existing Card
Play an Extra Card	Play an Extra Card	Play an Extra Card	Play an Extra Card
Move Another Space	Move Another Space	Move Another Space	
Puddleglum	Move an Existing Card	Move an Existing Card	Play an Extra Card

Play an Extra Card	*Play an Extra Card*	*Move Another Space*	*Move Another Space*
Move Another Space	*Move Another Space*	*Move Another Space*	

Prince	Move Another Space	Move Another Space	Move Another Space

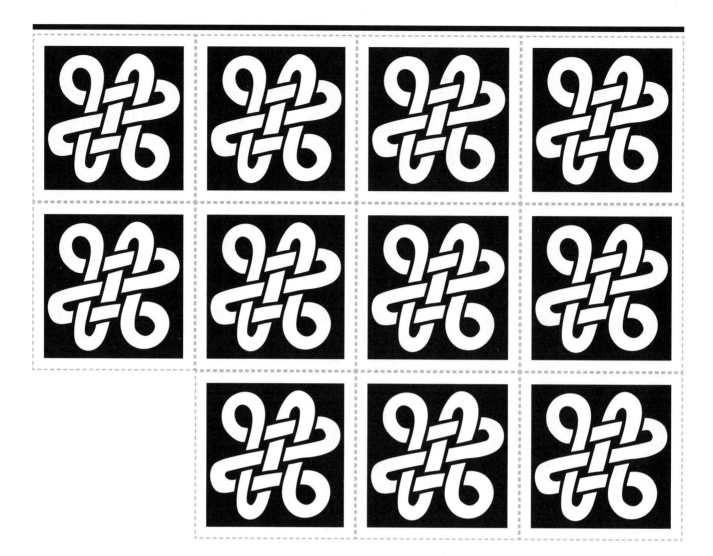

THE SILVER CHAIR
Chapter 6—"The Wild Waste Lands of the North"

1. What did Jill mistake for a pile of rocks, heather and birds' nests?

   _____

   _____

2. Why did the travellers find the game of cockshies so dangerous to them?

   _____

   _____

   _____

   _____

3. When Puddleglum, Scrubb and Jill were a mile a way past the gorge, what could they still hear?

   _____

   _____

   _____

4. What happened the only time they ever were noticed by a giant in Ettinsmoor?

   _____

   _____

   _____

5. Describe who they met on the other side of the giant's bridge.

   _____

   _____

   _____

   _____

   _____

6. What greetings were Puddleglum and the children to convey to the giants in Harfang?

    _____

    _____

    _____

7. Puddleglum did not trust the strangers they met. What did he imagine was inside the suit of armor?

    _____

    _____

    _____

8. What was the source of what might have been Puddleglum's and the children's first true quarrel?

    _____

    _____

    _____

9. What did Puddleglum insist on as his condition for agreeing to head for Harfang?

    _____

    _____

    _____

    _____

10. What caused Jill to stop rehearsing the signs and for them all to get more grumpy and snappy with each other?

    _____

    _____

    _____

THE SILVER CHAIR
Chapter 7—"The Hill of the Strange Trenches"

1. What made it hard to see that day?

   _____

   _____

   _____

2. When they were up on the tableland, what did Puddleglum ask Jill which she found annoying?

   _____

   _____

   _____

   _____

3. What distracted the children from following Puddleglum's suggestion of examining the tableland?

   _____

   _____

   _____

THE SILVER CHAIR
Chapter 7, Page 2

4. What about the appearance of the children did the Porter of Harfang's find so curious?

_____

_____

_____

5. What did the Porter offer to Puddleglum to drink from?

_____

_____

_____

6. Why was Jill unable to curtsey before the giant King and Queen?

_____

_____

_____

_____

THE SILVER CHAIR
Chapter 8—"The House of Harfang"

1. What did Jill do while they stood before the King and Queen?

   _____

   _____

2. Following her swim in the bath tub, what was Jill given to eat?

   _____

   _____

   _____

3. What annoying thing did the old Nurse keep doing?

   _____

   _____

   _____

4. Who appeared to Jill in her dream?

   _____

   _____

5. What did the three travellers see from the window seat in Jill's room?

   _____

   _____

   _____

6. What did Puddleglum guess were the intentions of the Lady of the Green Kirtle?

   _____

   _____

   _____

   _____

7. What did Scrubb propose as their only chance at escaping from Harfang?

    _____

    _____

    _____

8. How did Puddleglum and the children decide to act in order to gain access to the entire castle without arousing suspicion?

    _____

    _____

9. What were the plans of the giant King's court for the day before the Autumn Feast?

    _____

    _____

    _____

10. What did Jill ask the Queen which the courtiers found so funny?

    _____

    _____

    _____

    _____

    _____

    _____

THE SILVER CHAIR
Project—Cock-a-Leekie Soup

One of the courses for dinner after Jill's long, hot bath was Cock-a-Leekie Soup. Following is a recipe for this soup that you can try.

Ingredients

4 pounds boneless, skinless chicken thighs, cut into bite-size pieces

10 cups water

1 onion, chopped

1/3 cup barley

1 (10 1/2 ounce) can chicken broth

7 leeks, sliced

2 stalks celery, thickly sliced

1 sprig fresh thyme, chopped

1 tablespoon chopped fresh parsley

1 teaspoon salt

1/2 teaspoon ground black pepper

Directions

In a large pot over high heat, combine the chicken, water, onion and barley. Bring to a boil, reduce heat to low and simmer for 1 hour. Remove chicken, discard the bones and skin, chop meat into bite size pieces and return to the pot.

Add the chicken broth, leeks, celery, thyme, parsley, salt and ground black pepper. Simmer for 30 more minutes, or until all vegetables are tender. Makes 12 servings

THE SILVER CHAIR
Chapter 9—"How They Discovered Something Worth Knowing"

1. What important discovery did Jill make as she prattled and shook her curls all about the castle?

    _____

    _____

    _____

    _____

2. What made Puddleglum command the children to stop eating their lunch?

    _____

    _____

    _____

3. What did they read as they waited in the scullery for the giantess to fall asleep?

    _____

    _____

4. Why did the children's clothes present such a problem once they were outside of Harfang?

    _____

    _____

    _____

5. Why was the King so eager to catch the children?

    _____

    _____

    _____

6. What did the three travellers do as soon as Jill had crawled into the crevice to the right of the lowest step into the City Ruinous?

_____

_____

_____

7. What occurred as soon as Puddleglum suggested they return to be eaten by the giants instead of losing their way in the guts of a hill?

_____

_____

_____

8. What did Puddleglum lose in the darkness?

_____

_____

THE SILVER CHAIR
Chapter 10—"Travels Without the Sun"

1. Who was the first to greet the three travellers after their long fall?

   _____

   _____

   _____

2. What did the Warden say about those who go down into Dark Realm?

   _____

   _____

   _____

   _____

3. Why was Puddlgelum so glad to meet the earthmen?

   _____

   _____

   _____

4. Who was the enormous, noble, bearded man that they found sleeping, wrapped in silver light?

   _____

   _____

5. Whom did they meet in the City of the Underworld that they had met before?

   _____

   _____

   _____

6. What was the cause of Scrubb nearly being involved in a duel?

   _____

   _____

7. What did Puddleglum and the children learn was the history of the words in stone, "UNDER ME?"

_____

_____

_____

_____

_____

8. Why did Puddleglum not lose confidence in the message "UNDER ME" even after hearing of its history?

_____

_____

_____

_____

_____

9. What were the travellers told concerning the Queen's age and race?

_____

_____

_____

10. What had been promised to the Knight when he became king of the Overworld?

_____

_____

THE SILVER CHAIR
Chapter 11—"In the Dark Castle"

1. According to the Knight, how was he transformed each night?

   _____

   _____

   _____

2. Where was the Queen as the travellers dined with the Knight?

   _____

   _____

   _____

3. Why was the Knight told he could not speak when he rode in the Overworld?

   _____

   _____

   _____

   _____

4. In what was the Knight bound during his evening "fits?"

   _____

   _____

5. What did the Knight say which convinced Puddleglum and the children to free him?

   _____

   _____

   _____

   _____

6. What was the first thing the Knight did once he was free?

   _____

   _____

7. What was the Knight's true identity?

_____

_____

8. How long was the Knight in the power of the witch?

_____

_____

9. In the space provided below, draw your idea of what the magic chair looked like.

THE SILVER CHAIR
Chapter 12—"The Queen of the Underland"

1. What two things did Prince Rilian say when the Queen of the Underland unexpectedly arrived?

   _____

   _____

   _____

   _____

   _____

2. What two things did the Queen do in response to the Prince's declaration?

   _____

   _____

   _____

3. What did the Queen tell them about their memories of Narnia?

   _____

   _____

   _____

4. Of what did Puddleglum remind the Prince and the children which woke them?

   _____

   _____

5. Whose existence did Jill assert?

   _____

   _____

6. How did the Queen deny the existence of what Puddleglum and the children offered up as proof that there was more than just the Queen's world?

_____

_____

_____

7. What desperate, brave thing did Puddleglum do which broke the Queen's enchantment?

_____

_____

_____

8. What did the Queen do once her enchantments and arguments fail?

_____

_____

_____

9. How did they kill the Queen?

_____

_____

_____

10. Why did Rilian decide that his mother's death had been avenged?

_____

_____

_____

_____

THE SILVER CHAIR
Signs of the Silver Chair

A memory game for 2 to 4 players.

Components:

36 Matching Cards
8 Interrupt Cards

Of the Matching Cards, eight are related to the four signs Aslan gives to Jill: two of the cards are "old friend"; two of the cards are "giant city"; two of the cards are "stone with instructions"; two of the cards are "the Prince." The remaining twenty-eight Matching Cards are various things related to *The Silver Chair.*

Players begin the game with 2 Interrupt Cards each.

Shuffle the Matching Cards and lay them out in a 6x6 square, face down.

The youngest player goes first. Players take turns flipping two cards each; when a pair matches, they remove it from the board and keep it in a pile in front of them. If the pair does not match, flip them again so that they are face down.

The Interrupt Cards can be played by a player after an opponent has flipped one card, before that opponent flips the second card. For example: On her turn, Anna flips a card for "giant city." Brian plays an Interrupt Card. Brian can then flip the second card for Anna.
NOTE: If Brian makes a match, Anna gets the cards.

Once an Interrupt Card is played, it is out of the game. So each player can do this only twice during a game.

When all cards have been matched and removed from the board, add the scores. The eight cards related to the four signs are worth +2 points each (+4 points per pair). The Queen of the Underworld cards are worth -1 point each (-2 points per pair). Every other card is worth +1 point each (+2 points per pair).

The player with the highest score wins.

Game concept and rules by Erik Arneson.

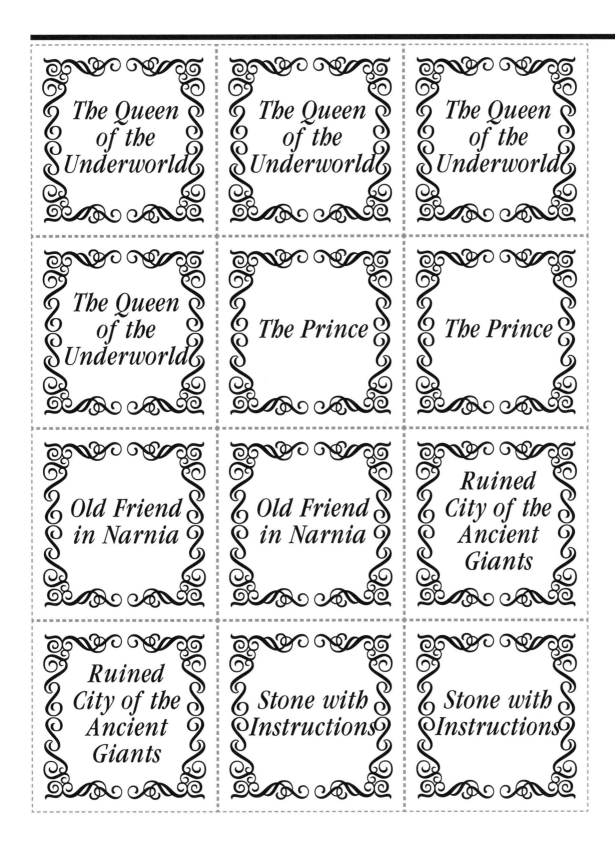

The Queen of the Underworld

The Queen of the Underworld

The Queen of the Underworld

The Queen of the Underworld

The Prince

The Prince

Old Friend in Narnia

Old Friend in Narnia

Ruined City of the Ancient Giants

Ruined City of the Ancient Giants

Stone with Instructions

Stone with Instructions

Scrubb

Scrubb

Jill

Jill

Puddleglum

Puddleglum

Glimfeather
the Owl

Glimfeather
the Owl

Aslan

Aslan

Land of
Bism

Land of
Bism

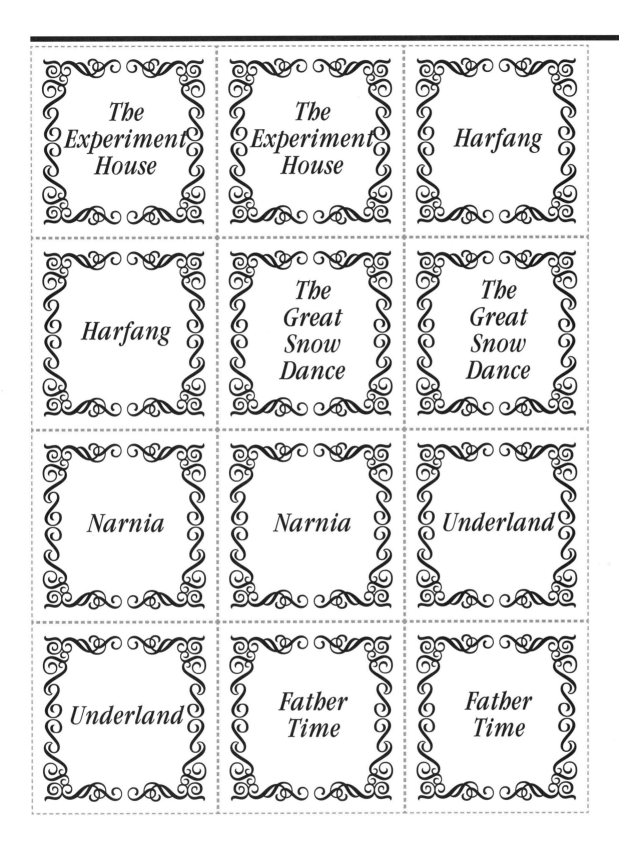

The
Experiment
House

The
Experiment
House

Harfang

Harfang

The
Great
Snow
Dance

The
Great
Snow
Dance

Narnia

Narnia

Underland

Underland

Father
Time

Father
Time

THE SILVER CHAIR
Chapter 13—"Underland Without the Queen"

1. What had the Witch done to her underground kingdom which was linked to her life?

   _____

   _____

   _____

2. What happened to Rilian's black shield?

   _____

   _____

   _____

3. What did Rilian tell them all to do before setting out into the streets?

   _____

   _____

4. Whom did Rilian wish to save before setting off for the higher grounds of the diggings?

   _____

   _____

   _____

5. What news caused the pigmy hippopatumus-faced gnome to declare his friendship to the Prince?

   _____

   _____

   _____

THE SILVER CHAIR
Chapter 14—"The Bottom of the World"

1. What was the name of the Really Deep Land—the country Golg was originally from?

   _____

   _____

2. How had the earthmen entered the service of the Witch?

   _____

   _____

   _____

3. What did the earthmen find so dreadful about the Queen's plan to take them "onto the outside of the world?"

   _____

   _____

   _____

4. What does the author use from our world to describe the brilliant colors of the Really Deep Land?

   _____

   _____

5. According to Golg, what lived in the fire-river?

   _____

   _____

6. What does Scrubb suggest Reepicheep would've said at the prospect of passing up adventures in the Really Deep Land?

   _____

   _____

   _____

7. How were diamonds and rubies different in the Really Deep Land than the ones in our world?

_____

_____

_____

8. Once they escaped past the rising water, what became their next concern?

_____

_____

_____

9. What did Puddleglum point out as the good thing about being trapped underground?

_____

_____

_____

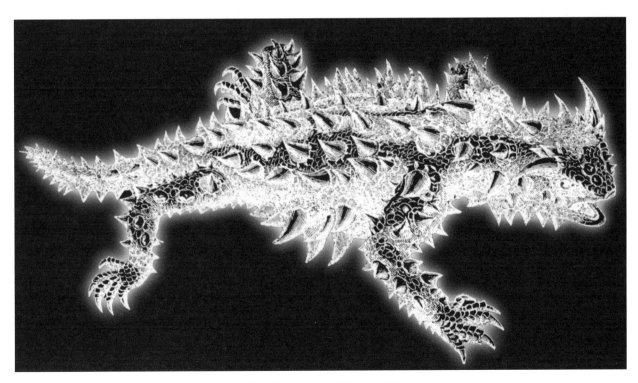

THE SILVER CHAIR
Chapter 15—"The Disapearance of Jill"

1. What happened to Jill that made Puddleglum say that he was born to be a misfit?

_____

_____

2. What were the fauns and dryads, encircled by the dwarves, involved in when Jill's head popped through the hole?

_____

_____

3. What did Scrubb do as soon as he was through the hole?

_____

_____

_____

4. How did the Fauns help the Dwarfs and Moles?

_____

_____

_____

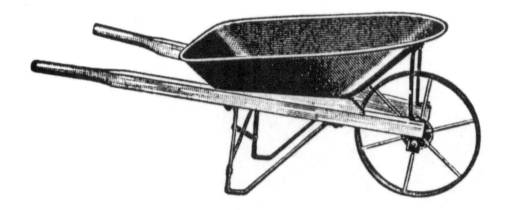

5. What did the Marsh-wiggle want to hear about instead of telling the Narnians his part of the adventure?

_____

_____

_____

_____

6. What lesson did the oldest Dwarf at the gathering distill about the sisterhood of Northern Witches?

_____

_____

_____

_____

THE SILVER CHAIR
Chapter 16—"The Healing of Harms"

1. What was for dinner the night before?

   _____

   _____

2. What was for breakfast that morning?

   _____

   _____

3. Why was it quite a serious thing to ask a centaur to stay with you for the weekend?

   _____

   _____

4. Why had Caspian returned to Narnia so soon after setting sail?

   _____

   _____

5. What rare (though rather uncomfortable) privilege was bestowed upon the children?

   _____

   _____

6. What sorts of things did the children learn about on their way to Cair Paravel?

   _____

   _____

7. What sad event occurred when Rilian was reunited with King Caspian?

   _____

   _____

8. What remained on the Mountain of Aslan after the Lion had blown away the ship, the dead King and the castle in Narnia?

    _____

    _____

9. What did Aslan command Eustace to do as they wept by stream where the dead King Caspian lay?

    _____

    _____

    _____

10. What happened in the end to the Head of the Experiment House?

    _____

    _____

    _____

11. How did Jill make use of her Narnian clothes in our world?

    _____

    _____

    _____

12. What became of the opening to what was the Queen of the Underland's realm?

    _____

    _____

    _____

THE SILVER CHAIR
Project—Baked Apples

She had a vague impression of Dwarfs crowding around the fire with frying-pans rather bigger than themselves, and the hissing, and delicious smell of sausages, and more, and more, and more sausages. And not wretched sausages half full of bread and soya bean either, but real meaty, spicy ones, fat and piping hot and burst and just the tiniest bit burnt. And great mugs of frothy chocolate, and roast potatoes and roast chestnuts, and baked apples with raisins stuck in where the cores had been, and then ices just to freshen you up after all the hot things.
—The Silver Chair

Ingredients (Per student)

1 small apple (cored, and peeled 1/3 of the way down)

1 tablespoon raisins

1 teaspoon lemon juice

1/2 teaspoon honey

A couple drops of rum flavoring

A dash of cinnamon

1 teaspoon water

Directions

Oven 350 degrees F. Combine all of the ingredients except the water and apple. Stuff this into the apple. Place the water in the bottom of an ovenproof custard cup, put the apple in the cup. Cover the apple with foil and bake for 35-45 minutes.

Microwave method: Cover with plastic wrap and cook for 2 minutes on high, check to see if it is done, turn and continue to heat in 1 minute increments, turning each minute, until the apple is soft and cooked.

THE LAST BATTLE
Chapter 1—"By Caldron Pool"

1. What trait did the Ape possess which made him able to get the Donkey to do whatever he wanted him to do?

    _____

    _____

    _____

2. What did Puzzle fish out of Caldron Pool for Shift?

    _____

    _____

3. What did Puzzle want them to do with this thing that had been discarded months before in the Western Wild?

    _____

    _____

4. What did Shift occupy himself with while Puzzle was off at the market in Chippingford?

    _____

    _____

    _____

5. After dressing Puzzle up, for whom did Shift say people might mistake the Donkey?

    _____

    _____

6. What reason did the Ape give to propose that tricking Narnians was a good thing?

    _____

    _____

    _____

THE LAST BATTLE
Chapter 1, Page 2

7. What did Shift say was
   wrong with Narnia?

   _____

   _____

   _____

   _____

   _____

8. What did Puzzle interpret
   the thunderclap to mean?

   _____

   _____

   _____

   _____

   _____

   _____

9. What did the Ape interpret the thunderclap to mean?

   _____

   _____

   _____

   _____

   _____

THE LAST BATTLE
Chapter 2—"The Rashness of the King"

1. What had King Tirian and Jewel the Unicorn done for each other in the wars?

   _____

   _____

2. What news kept the King from wanting to work or sport that pleasant spring day?

   _____

   _____

3. What bad news did Roonwit bring to the King?

   _____

   _____

4. What was said in the old stories which made Jewel and Tirian think that Aslan would act in a way other than how the stars foretold?

   _____

   _____

   _____

5. Why did the Dryad cry out to the King for Justice, Aid and Protection?

   _____

   _____

   _____

6. What caused the Dryad to vanish?

   _____

   _____

THE LAST BATTLE
Chapter 2, Page 2

7. What did Tirian send Roonwit to fetch?

_____

_____

_____

8. What struck the King oddly about the crowd of Beasts and Men he saw tearing down the trees?

_____

_____

_____

9. What shocking discovering did Jewel and Tirian make about the creature they found two Calormen beating?

_____

_____

_____

10. What rash act do the King and the Unicorn commit?

_____

_____

_____

THE LAST BATTLE
Chapter 3—"The Ape in Its Glory"

1. What was it that Tirian described as the sun rising one day as a black sun, and Jewel
    described like drinking water only to find it is *dry* water?

    _____

    _____

    _____

2. What was done to the two friends when they returned and gave themselves up to the
    foul-smelling Calormen?

    _____

    _____

    _____

3. Describe the appearance of "the mouthpiece of Aslan."

    _____

    _____

    _____

    _____

    _____

4. What other business did Shift attend to before dealing with the King and the Unicorn?

    _____

    _____

    _____

5. What claim did Shift make about himself along with claiming to be hundreds of years old and very wise?

_____

_____

6. What were some of the benefits to Narnia Shift says would be the result of the Talking Animals being sold into slavery?

_____

_____

_____

7. What did Shift say about Aslan to explain how Tash and Aslan could be friends?

_____

_____

_____

_____

8. What was the only talking animal which listened to all the lies of the Ape calmly?

_____

_____

9. What did Tirian do which got him punched, kicked, and tied to a tree?

_____

_____

_____

THE LAST BATTLE
Chapter 4—"What Happened That Night"

1. What worried the King most about being tied to the ash tree?

   _____

   _____

   _____

2. What did Mice, Moles and a Rabbit serve the King for supper?

   _____

   _____

   _____

3. What did Tirian remember that made him realize that the "lion" he saw come out of the stable was not Aslan—that it was all a trick?

   _____

   _____

   _____

4. Tirian prayed to Aslan and requested what?

   _____

   _____

   _____

   _____

5. Decribe what the King saw in his dream.

_____

_____

_____

_____

_____

_____

6. Though Tirian could not speak, who spoke to the him in the dream?

_____

_____

_____

THE LAST BATTLE
Chapter 5—"How Help Came to the King"

1. Who "bumped" into Narnia to aid the King?

   _____

   _____

2. How much time had passed in our world for the visitors to Narnia since they had seen the vision of Tirian?

   _____

   _____

3. What was offered to Tirian for his breakfast?

   _____

   _____

4. What was Tirian's destination for them as they marched?

   _____

   _____

5. Why had Digory organized a meeting of the friends of Narnia?

   _____

   _____

6. How did Peter and Edmund deal with the possibility of getting caught as they went to dig up the Rings?

   _____

   _____

   _____

7. How did Tirian's two companions end up getting into Narnia?

_____

_____

_____

8. Besides basic food and fresh weapons, what was the King particularly pleased to find in the square tower?

_____

_____

_____

9. What had the children been practicing since they were last in Narnia?

_____

_____

10. After sitting down to dinner, what did Tirian lament that the towers were missing?

_____

_____

THE LAST BATTLE
Chapter 6—"A Good Night's Work"

1. Though Tirian found Jill was not bad at archery, what did the King need to teach Eustace how to do?

   _____

   _____

2. What was the first thing the three planned to do before joining the army Roonwit was bringing from Cair Paravel?

   _____

   _____

3. What is the name of Narnia's North Star?

   _____

   _____

4. How did the King leave the sentry he found guarding that night?

_____

_____

_____

5. What did Jill do when they were at the stable?

_____

_____

_____

6. What did Tirian want to do, but was stopped by Jill?

_____

_____

_____

7. Why was the King eager to meet up with the Dwarfs?

_____

_____

_____

THE LAST BATTLE
Chapter 7—"Mainly About Dwarfs"

1. What did the King and Eustace do to two of the Calormen leading the captive Dwarfs?

   _____

   _____

   _____

2. When the Dwarfs demanded to see the true Aslan what did the King say that was "a false move?"

   _____

   _____

   _____

3. Whom did the Dwarfs say they were going to side with instead of the King?

   _____

   _____

4. What unexpected result came from the Ape setting up of a false Aslan?

   _____

   _____

   _____

5. Who was the only Dwarf to leave the others to join with the King?

   _____

   _____

6. What things did the noble Unicorn kindly talk about with the Donkey?

   _____

   _____

   _____

7. What deceitful tale had Ginger told the
   animals at the stable to cover up the dis-
   appearance of the King?

   _____

   _____

   _____

   _____

   _____

   _____

   _____

8. What did Ginger the Cat clarify as to the meaning behind the Tarkaan's statement that
   Aslan meant *no more* than Tash?

   _____

   _____

   _____

   _____

THE LAST BATTLE
Chapter 8—"What News the Eagle Brought"

1. Describe the appearance of Tash.

   _____

   _____

   _____

   _____

   _____

2. Why did Tirian and the others not simply attack the thirty Calormen who were at the stable?

   _____

   _____

   _____

   _____

3. What mistake about the history of Narnia did Jill make which the Unicorn corrected?

   _____

   _____

4. What did Jill learn about Swanwhite the Queen?

   _____

   _____

   _____

   _____

5. How were the Lone Islands joined into the Narnian realm?

    _____

    _____

    _____

6. Who brought the news to Tirian that made the King utter, "Narnia is no more."

    _____

    _____

7. What two terrible tidings did this messenger bring?

    _____

    _____

    _____

8. What two-fold message did Roonwit send to the King?

    _____

    _____

    _____

    _____

    _____

THE LAST BATTLE
Chapter 8, Project

Compose a Narnian marching song to go with the refrain Tirian hummed:

Ho, rumble, rumble, rumble,
Rumble drum belaboured.

_____

_____

_____

_____

_____

_____

_____

_____

_____

_____

_____

_____

_____

_____

_____

_____

THE LAST BATTLE
The Badger and the Unicorn *Trivia Game*

"But the Unicorn explained . . . [that] there were hundreds and thousands of years when peaceful King followed peaceful King till you could hardly remember their names or count their numbers, and there was really hardly anything to put into History Books."

"'I tell you, we don't change, we beasts,' said Trufflehunter. 'We don't forget.'"

A trivia game with auctions for 2 to 5 players or teams.

Equipment

Trivia cards—each card has two questions: Badger (easy, 1 point) and Unicorn (difficult, 2 points). There are blanks included for the students to create their own additional questions.

1 six-sided die

10 auction counters per player or team (pennies, or just a pencil and paper)

1 ten-second timer or stopwatch (or just someone who can count to 10)

Gameplay:

2 PLAYERS

Shuffle the cards and deal 10 to each player. Players take turn asking each other questions, first the easy question and then the difficult question (so each player will try to answer 20 questions, 10 Badger and 10 Unicorn). The winner is the player with the most points. If a game ends in a tie, the players ask each other difficult questions in sudden-death style until there is a winner.

3 TO 5 PLAYERS

Shuffle the cards and deal 7 to each player or team. (If you discover that this makes the game too long or too short, simply adjust the number of cards.)

Each player or team begins with 10 auction counters.

Randomly choose a player/team to ask the first question. That player/team chooses which of the questions will be asked—Badger or Unicorn—and announces the decision.

The other players/teams secretly prepare a bid for the right to answer the question. They may bid any number of auction counters, from zero up to the total they currently own. All bids are revealed simultaneously.

The player/team who bids the highest wins the right to answer the question. The player/team asking the question reads it out loud, and the winning bidder has 10 seconds to answer it. If it is answered correctly, the player/team that answered it wins the appropriate number of points (1 or 2).

Continued after trivia cards

B: In *The Magician's Nephew*, what had Digory been doing just before he met Polly?
Crying

U: In *The Magician's Nephew*, what was the name of Uncle Andrew's godmother?
Mrs. Lefay

B: In *The Magician's Nephew*, what gift did Uncle Andrew give to Polly before she left his room?
A yellow ring

U: In *The Magician's Nephew*, where did the box Uncle Andrew was given come from originally?
Atlantis

B: In *The Magician's Nephew*, what did Uncle Andrew first send to the Wood Between the Worlds?
A guinea pig

U: In *The Magician's Nephew*, what was odd about the light in Charn?
It was a dull red light

B: In *The Magician's Nephew*, where did the yellow rings initially take Digory and Polly?
The Wood Between the Worlds

U: In *The Magician's Nephew*, where was the message: "Make your choice, adventurous Stranger . . ."
On a square pillar in Charn

B: In *The Magician's Nephew*, what did the Queen wrongly assume about Uncle Andrew?
That he was a great Magician king

U: In *The Magician's Nephew*, how did Jadis say that she defeated her sister?
Using the Deplorable Word

B: In *The Magician's Nephew*, how did the Queen, or Witch, follow Digory and Polly into the Woods?
Holding onto Polly's Hair

U: In *The Magician's Nephew*, what was the first thing sung into existence?
Stars

B: In *The Magician's Nephew*, how did the Queen, or Witch, follow Digory and Polly into our world?
Holding onto Digory's ear

U: In *The Magician's Nephew*, what was responsible for singing everything into existence?
Aslan

B: In *The Magician's Nephew*, what effect did the Wood Between the Worlds have on Jadis?
It weakened her

U: In *The Magician's Nephew*, what happened to the animals that the Lion breathed on?
They became talking animals

B: In *The Magician's Nephew*, where did Letty think Jadis was from?
The circus

U: In *The Magician's Nephew*, what did the Witch break off to bludgeon the chief policeman?
One of the cross-bars of a lamp-post

B: In *The Magician's Nephew*, what did Aslan make the Cabby and his wife?
The first King and Queen in Narnia

U: In *The Magician's Nephew*, who was the first joke?
The Jackdaw

B: In *The Magician's Nephew*, what was it about the Tree of Protection which would protect Narnia?
The smell of the tree

U: In *The Magician's Nephew*, who became the first king of Archenland?
King Frank's second son

B: In *The Magician's Nephew*, what did Aslan send Digory to get?
An apple

U: In *The Magician's Nephew*, what white stuff did Strawberry want when he gave a ride to Digory and Polly?
Sugar cubes

B: In *The Magician's Nephew*, what did the animals name Uncle Andrew?
Brandy

U: In *The Magician's Nephew*, what became of the tree that Digory planted in our world?
It was made into a wardrobe

B: In *The Lion, the Witch and the Wardrobe*, what were the names of the four Pevensie children?
Peter, Susan, Edmund, Lucy

U: In *The Lion, the Witch and the Wardrobe*, why did the Pevensie children go to stay in the country?
World War II air raids over London

U: In *The Lion, the Witch and the Wardrobe*, how did the children get into Narnia?
A wardrobe

U: In *The Lion, the Witch and the Wardrobe*, what was in the room with the dead-blue bottle?
A wardrobe

B: In *The Lion, the Witch and the Wardrobe*, what did Lucy find in the back of the wardrobe?
A lamppost in the woods

U: In *The Lion, the Witch and the Wardrobe*, what were they doing when Edmund went first to Narnia?
Playing Hide and Seek

B: In *The Lion, the Witch and the Wardrobe*, what kind of creature did Lucy first meet in Narnia?
A Faun

U: In *The Lion, the Witch and the Wardrobe*, where was the book *Nymphs and Their Ways* found?
Tumnus' bookshelf

B: In *The Lion, the Witch and the Wardrobe*, what was the name of the Faun Lucy first met?
Mr. Tumnus

U: In *The Lion, the Witch and the Wardrobe*, what did the Witch pay Tumnus to do?
Kidnap humans

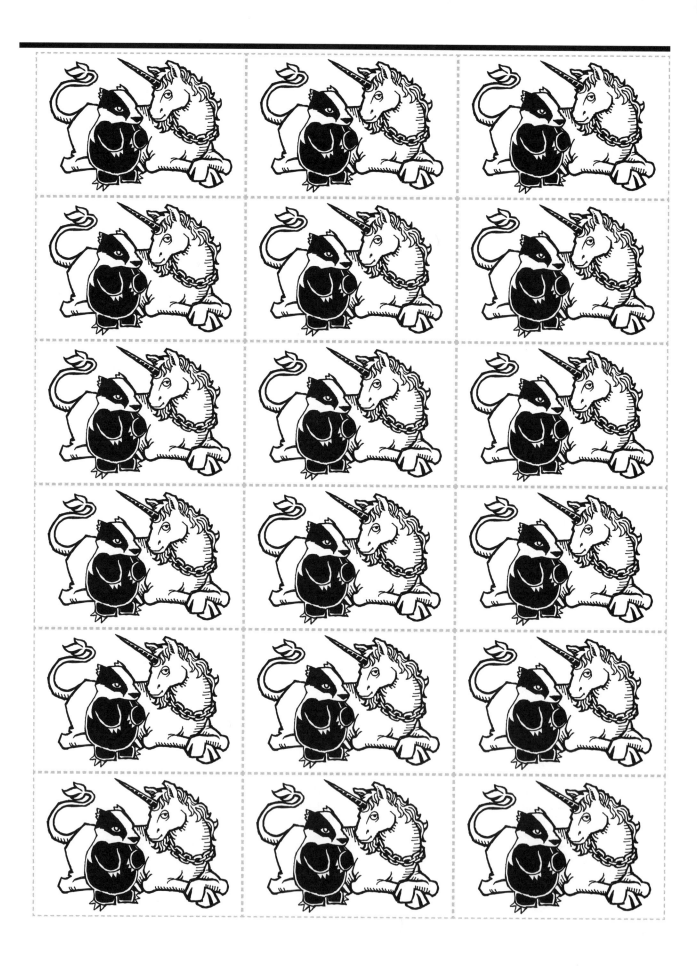

B: In *The Lion, the Witch and the Wardrobe*, what reward was given to those who caught the white stag?
Wishes

U: In *The Lion, the Witch and the Wardrobe*, where was giant Rumblebuffin found?
The castle of the White Witch

B: In *The Lion, the Witch and the Wardrobe*, where was the Queen's house located?
Between two hills

U: In *The Lion, the Witch and the Wardrobe*, what is the name of the captain of the secret police?
Fenris Ulf or Maugrim

B: In *The Lion, the Witch and the Wardrobe*, what was Mrs. Beaver doing when the children arrived?
Sewing

B: In *The Lion, the Witch and the Wardrobe*, whose side did the man-headed bull join?
Aslan's

B: In *The Lion, the Witch and the Wardrobe*, what was the name of the housekeeper?
Mrs. Macready

U: In *The Lion, the Witch and the Wardrobe*, what did the children call Digory?
Professor

B: In *The Lion, the Witch and the Wardrobe*, what presents did Lucy receive?
A diamond cordial and dagger

U: Who was the son of the Emperor-beyond-the-Sea?
Aslan

B: In *The Lion, the Witch and the Wardrobe*, who followed Aslan back to the Stone Table?
Susan and Lucy

U: In *The Lion, the Witch and the Wardrobe*, what time did the Stone Table crack?
Sunrise

B: In *The Lion, the Witch and the Wardrobe*, what had the White Witch done to Narnia?
Made it winter and never Christmas

U: In *The Lion, the Witch and the Wardrobe*, what was given to Mrs. Beaver by Father Christmas?
A new sewing machine

B: In *The Lion, the Witch and the Wardrobe*, what did the children take from the house into Narnia?
Fur coats

U: In *The Lion, the Witch and the Wardrobe*, of what crime was Faun Tumnus accused?
Fraternizing with humans

B: In *The Lion, the Witch and the Wardrobe*, what did the White Witch do to Mr. Tumnus?
Turned him to stone

U: Who was the father of Aslan?
The great Emperor-Beyond-the-Sea

B: In *The Lion, the Witch and the Wardrobe*, what presents did Peter receive?
A shield and sword

U: In *The Lion, the Witch and the Wardrobe*, what carried Aslan's crown and standard?
Leopards

B: In *The Lion, the Witch and the Wardrobe*, what did Peter do for which Aslan knighted him?
Saved Susan by killing a wolf

U: In *The Lion, the Witch and the Wardrobe*, what did Aslan command Peter to never forget to do?
Clean his sword

B: In *The Lion, the Witch and the Wardrobe*, who removed the cords that bound Aslan's dead body?
Mice

U: In *The Lion, the Witch and the Wardrobe*, who sang in honor of the new Kings and Queens?
Mermen and mermaids

B: In *The Lion, the Witch and the Wardrobe*, what token did Lucy leave with the Faun?
Handkerchief

U: In *The Lion, the Witch and the Wardrobe*, what did Edmund eat when he was first with the Witch?
Turkish Delight

B: In *The Lion, the Witch and the Wardrobe*, where did the Beaver take the children for dinner?
His dam/den

U: In *The Lion, the Witch and the Wardrobe*, what did Peter and Mr. Beaver get for dinner?
Trout

B: In *The Lion, the Witch and the Wardrobe*, when Edmund left the beavers, what did he leave behind?
Fur coat

U: In *The Lion, the Witch and the Wardrobe*, what did Edmund decide was to be his first act as King?
Make some decent roads

B: In *The Lion, the Witch and the Wardrobe*, what presents did Susan receive?
A bow and arrows, horn

U: In *The Lion, the Witch and the Wardrobe*, what gift did Susan use first?
Her horn

B: In *The Lion, the Witch and the Wardrobe*, how does the Dwarf propose to keep the thrones empty?
Kill Edmund

U: In *The Lion, the Witch and the Wardrobe*, where was the Deep Magic engraved?
The Stone Table

B: In *The Lion, the Witch and the Wardrobe*, who smashed the wand?
Edmund

U: In *The Lion, the Witch and the Wardrobe*, what did Aslan say at the children's coronation?
"Once a king or queen in Narnia, always a king or queen."

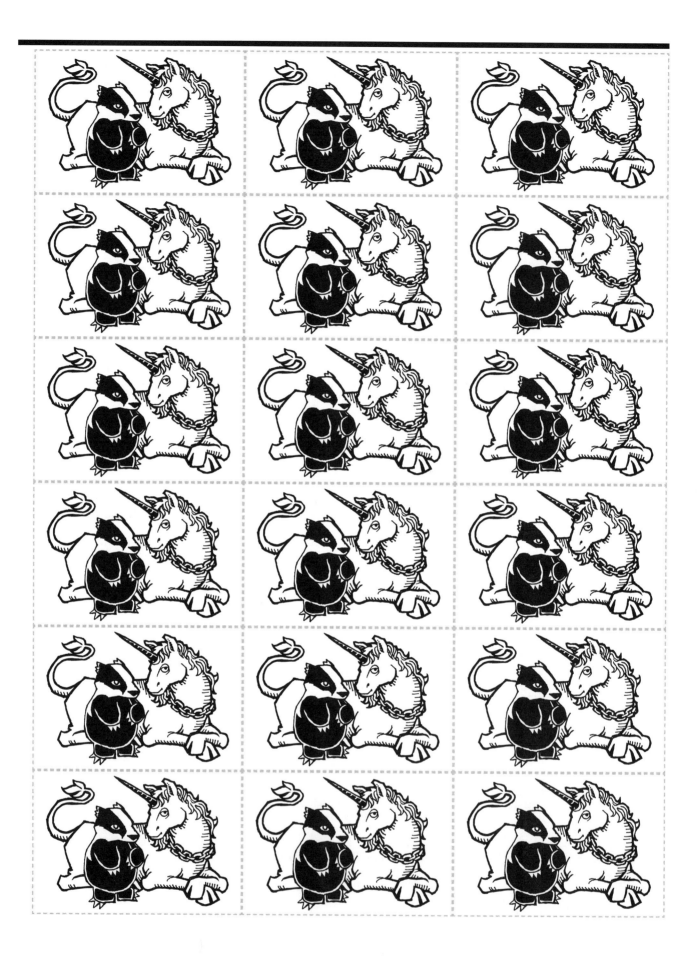

B: In *The Horse and His Boy*, what was the Horse's name?
Bree

U: In *The Horse and His Boy*, what did Arsheesh do to earn a living?
He was a fisherman

B: In *The Horse and His Boy*, what was Aravis' horse's name?
Hwin

U: In *The Horse and His Boy*, how were Bree and Hwin related?
Second cousins once removed

B: In *The Horse and His Boy*, who kept Aravis from suicide?
Hwin

U: In *The Horse and His Boy*, what did the soldier at the gate to Tashbaan accuse Shasta of doing?
Using his master's saddle-horse for pack work

B: In *The Horse and His Boy*, what "friend" did Aravis see in Tashbaan?
Tarkheena Lasaraleen

U: In *The Horse and His Boy*, how did Aravis know Lasaraleen?
They had stayed at the same houses and been to the same parties

B: In *The Horse and His Boy*, what was the name of Shasta's human companion?
Aravis

U: In *The Horse and His Boy*, how was Aravis like a classic fairy tale princess?
She had an evil stepmother

B: In *The Horse and His Boy*, as Aravis was being attacked by a lion, what did Shasta do?
He shouted at the lion, "Go home!"

U: In *The Horse and His Boy*, how many scratches had the lion drawn across the back of Aravis?
Ten

B: In *The Horse and His Boy*, what scratched Shasta among the Tombs outside of Tashbaan?
A large green-eyed cat

U: In *The Horse and His Boy*, why did Lasaraleen and Aravis have to hide behind a couch?
They almost ran into the Tisroc

B: In *The Horse and His Boy*, what was the reason for the Narnians visiting Tashbaan?
Queen Susan was considering an offer of marriage

U: In *The Horse and His Boy*, who did Queen Susan think Shasta was?
Prince Corin of Archenland

B: In *The Horse and His Boy*, what was the name of the boy Shasta met in Tashbaan?
Prince Corin

U: In *The Horse and His Boy*, what occurred the day before Calormen ambassadors came to Cair Paravel?
Moles planted an orchard

B: In *The Horse and His Boy*, where did King Lune live?
Anvard

U: In *The Horse and His Boy*, who kidnapped Prince Cor as a child?
Lord Chancellor Bar

B: In *The Horse and His Boy*, who taught Shasta how to ride?
Bree

U: In *The Horse and His Boy*, what unique battle equipment did the giants carry?
Heavy, horrid, spiked knee-high boots

B: In *The Horse and His Boy*, who taught Shasta how to use reins?
Prince Corin

U: In *The Horse and His Boy*, how was the Hermit able to see the battle?
By looking into a pool in his hermitage

B: In *The Horse and His Boy*, who did King Lune first think Shasta was when he met him?
His son, Prince Corin

U: In *The Horse and His Boy*, why did Rabadash repeatedly kick the Grand Vizier?
For quoting proverbs at him

B: In *The Horse and His Boy*, why was Shasta not able to take turns walking across the desert?
He had no shoes to wear

U: In *The Horse and His Boy*, what landmark signified the entrance into Archenland from the south?
Winding Arrow

B: In *The Horse and His Boy*, what did the Calormen make at Anvard?
A ram

U: In *The Horse and His Boy*, what did Rabadash yell just before he was unintentionally hung on a hook on the wall?
"The bolt of Tash falls from above."

B: In *The Horse and His Boy*, how many lions attacked Shasta?
One

U: In *The Horse and His Boy*, what tales were told in Calormen about Aslan?
That Aslan was a demon who went around in the shape of a lion

B: In *The Horse and His Boy*, what was on Narnia's flag?
A red rampant lion on a green field

U: In *The Horse and His Boy*, who took the news of the invasion to Cair Paravel?
A stag named Chervy

B: In *The Horse and His Boy*, what Narnian king went to help Anvard?
Edmund

U: In *The Horse and His Boy*, why was Queen Lucy unable to use her cordial to heal Thornbut?
King Peter prohibited Lucy from carrying it commonly to wars

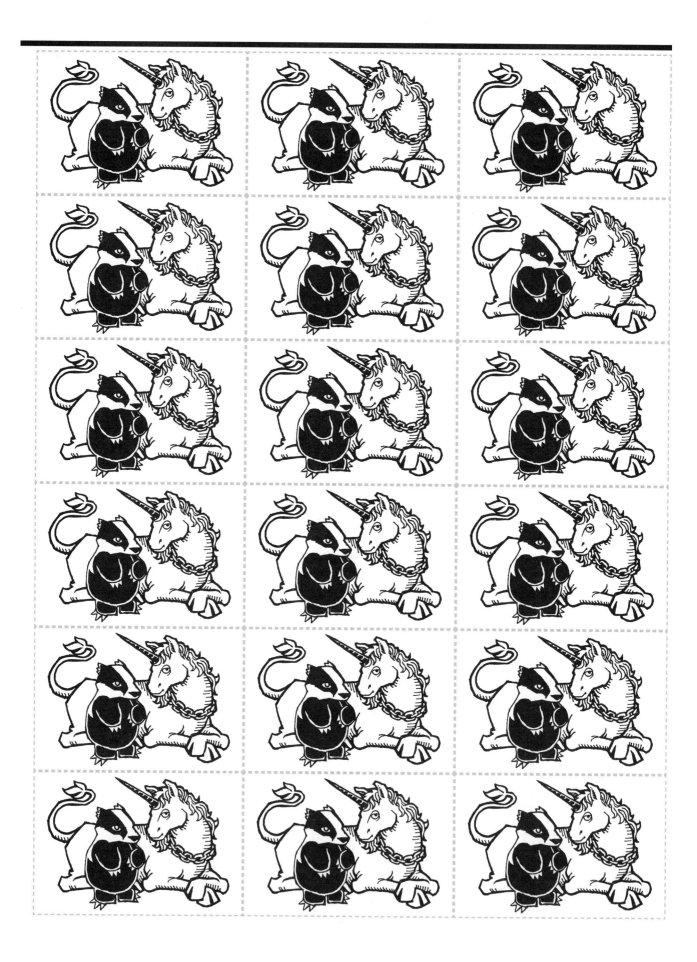

B: In *The Horse and His Boy,* what did the Hermit offer them to drink?
Goat's milk

U: In *The Horse and His Boy,* for what was King Olven famous?
Fighting the two-headed giant Pire, turning him into stone and winning the hand of Lady Liln

B: In *The Horse and His Boy,* who was Aravis supposed to marry?
The Grand Vizier

U: In *The Horse and His Boy,* what was Corin Thunder-Fist's greatest exploit?
Boxing a lapsed talking bear

B: In *The Horse and His Boy,* what doom—or punishment—was inflicted on the Prince Rabadash?
He was changed into a donkey

U: In *The Horse and His Boy,* what was the other name for Rabadash the Peacemaker?
Rabadash the Ridiculous

B: In *The Horse and His Boy,* who did Prince Cor marry?
Aravis

U: In *The Horse and His Boy,* what famous heir did King Cor and Queen Aravis produce?
Ram the Great

B: In *The Horse and His Boy,* what was the name of Shasta's real father?
King Lune

U: In *The Horse and His Boy,* who welcomed Aravis and helped her to settle in to Anvard?
Queen Lucy

B: In *Prince Caspian: The Return to Narnia,* to what defensible place did the Old Narnians fall back?
Aslan's How

U: In *Prince Caspian: The Return to Narnia,* how long did the Pevensies think they had been out of Narnia?
One Year

B: In *Prince Caspian: The Return to Narnia,* where are the children when drawn back into Narnia?
Railway station

U: In *Prince Caspian: The Return to Narnia,* who saves Trumpkin from drowning?
Susan

B: In *Prince Caspian: The Return to Narnia,* what did Susan find in the castle ruins?
A gold chess-knight

U: In *Prince Caspian: The Return to Narnia,* who did Aslan tell that they will not return to Narnia?
Peter and Susan

B: In *Prince Caspian: The Return to Narnia,* who replaced Caspian's nurse?
Doctor Cornelius

U: In *Prince Caspian: The Return to Narnia,* who killed Caspian IX?
Miraz

B: In *Prince Caspian: The Return to Narnia,* what drew the children back into Narnia?
The Horn of Susan

U: In *Prince Caspian: The Return to Narnia,* why did the Bulgy Bears wish to delay the Council of War?
They wanted to eat

B: In *Prince Caspian: The Return to Narnia,* what did they eat for supper in the ruinous castle?
Apples

U: In *Prince Caspian: The Return to Narnia,* who was the last to feel drawn into Narnia?
Susan

B: In *Prince Caspian: The Return to Narnia,* what was missing from the treasure room in Cair Paravel?
Susan's Horn

U: In *Prince Caspian: The Return to Narnia,* what were the names of Prince Caspian's uncle and aunt?
Miraz and Prunaprismia

B: In *Prince Caspian: The Return to Narnia,* who first taught Caspian about the Old Narnians?
His nurse

U: In *Prince Caspian: The Return to Narnia,* what were Tarva and Alambil?
Planets

B: In *Prince Caspian: The Return to Narnia,* what did Cornelius call the reign of the Pevensie children?
The Golden Age of Narnia

U: In *Prince Caspian: The Return to Narnia,* what rare gift did Cornelius give to Caspian?
The Horn of Queen Susan

B: In *Prince Caspian: The Return to Narnia,* who betrayed Caspian to his Uncle Miraz?
His horse, Destrier

U: In *Prince Caspian: The Return to Narnia,* what was the name of Caspian's horse?
Destrier

B: In *Prince Caspian: The Return to Narnia,* over what was Aslan's How built?
The Stone Table

U: In *Prince Caspian: The Return to Narnia,* what did squirrels think showed bad manners?
To watch a squirrel get his nuts

B: In *Prince Caspian: The Return to Narnia,* who won the match between Edmund and Trumpkin?
Edmund

U: In *Prince Caspian: The Return to Narnia,* Cornelius was half human and half what?
Dwarf

B: In *Prince Caspian: The Return to Narnia,* what kind of match did Susan have with the Dwarf?
Archery

U: In *Prince Caspian: The Return to Narnia,* what did "D.L.F." stand for?
Dear Little Friend

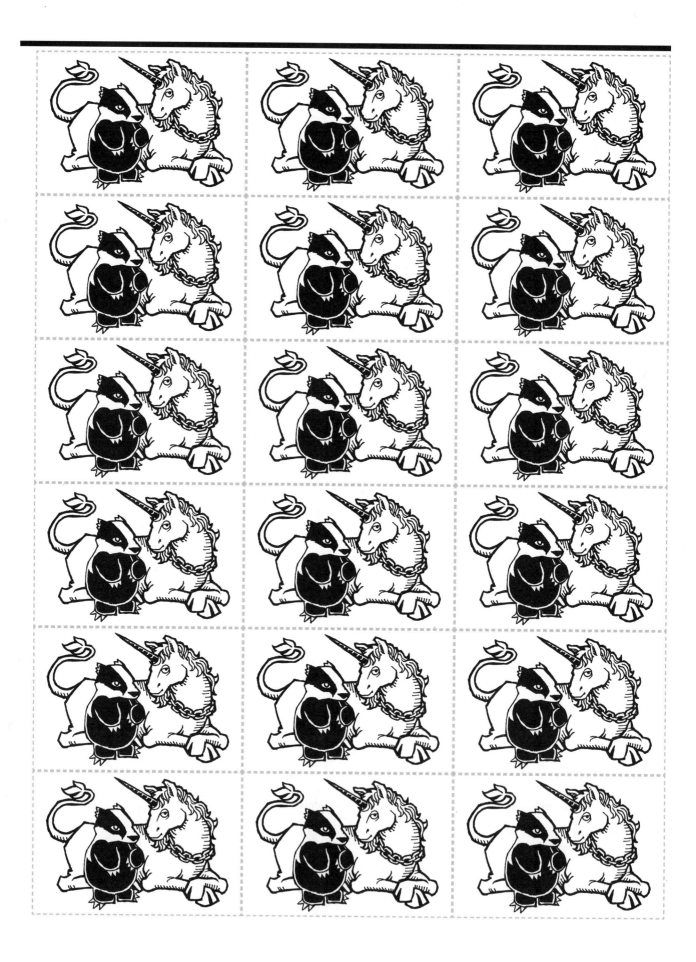

B: In *Prince Caspian: The Return to Narnia*, who destroyed the bridge at Beruna?
Bacchus

U: In *Prince Caspian: The Return to Narnia*, what grew madly during the Romp?
Vines and grapes

B: In *Prince Caspian: The Return to Narnia*, what supposedly filled the "Black Woods?"
Ghosts

U: In *Prince Caspian: The Return to Narnia*, what old enemy did Nikabrik wish to call on for aid?
The White Witch

B: In *Prince Caspian: The Return to Narnia*, off of what did Silenus fall?
A donkey

U: In *Prince Caspian: The Return to Narnia*, for what Talking animals' extinction did Nikabrik credit the Queen?
Beavers

B: In *Prince Caspian: The Return to Narnia*, who wakes the trees?
Aslan

U: In *Prince Caspian: The Return to Narnia*, who really killed Miraz?
Glozelle

B: In *Prince Caspian: The Return to Narnia*, when Reepicheep appeared before Aslan, what was he missing?
His tail

U: In *Prince Caspian: The Return to Narnia*, what did Aslan do throughout the night?
Gazed with joy on the Moon

B: In *Prince Caspian: The Return to Narnia*, what did Edmund accidentally leave in Narnia?
His new torch—his flashlight

U: In *Prince Caspian: The Return to Narnia*, of what were the Telmars descendants?
Pirates

B: In *The Voyage of the* Dawn Treader, what was the name of the Pevensie's cousin?
Eustace (Clarence Scrubb)

U: In *The Voyage of the* Dawn Treader, where did the painting of the Dawn Treader hang?
Upstairs in Lucy's room

B: During *The Voyage of the* Dawn Treader, where was Susan?
America

U: In *The Voyage of the* Dawn Treader, what was the name of the Dawn Treader's captain?
Lord Drinian

B: In *The Voyage of the* Dawn Treader, where was it that Reepicheep hoped to reach?
Aslan's Country

U: In *The Voyage of the* Dawn Treader, what did the Duke of Galma want King Caspian to do?
Marry his daughter

B: In *The Voyage of the* Dawn Treader, what did Lucy drink when she first arrived on the ship?
Hot spiced wine

U: In *The Voyage of the* Dawn Treader, how was Lucy able to cure Eustace of his seasickness?
A drop from her diamond cordial

B: In *The Voyage of the* Dawn Treader, what island was closest to Cair Paravel?
Galma

U: In *The Voyage of the* Dawn Treader, where did the lookout stand?
On a shelf inside the dragon head

B: During *The Voyage of the* Dawn Treader, where did they run into slavers?
The Lone Islands or Felimath

U: In *The Voyage of the* Dawn Treader, who wanted to visit Felimath?
Lucy

B: In *The Voyage of the* Dawn Treader, what was the name of the Governor of the Lone Islands?
Gumpas

U: In *The Voyage of the* Dawn Treader, how much did Lord Bern pay for Caspian?
150 crescents

B: In *The Voyage of the* Dawn Treader, who was Pug unable to sell?
Eustace

U: In *The Voyage of the* Dawn Treader, what was one hundred and fifty years overdue to Narnia?
Tribute

B: In *The Voyage of the* Dawn Treader, who kept Eustace from stealing water?
Reepicheep

U: In *The Voyage of the* Dawn Treader, what drove Eustace into the dragon's cave?
A thunderstorm

B: In *The Voyage of the* Dawn Treader, what did Eustace slip on in the dragon's cave?
A jewel-encrusted bracelet

U: In *The Voyage of the* Dawn Treader, what was the first thing Eustace liked in being a dragon?
He could fly

B: In *The Voyage of the* Dawn Treader, what did the serpent break?
The stern of the Dawn Treader

U: In *The Voyage of the* Dawn Treader, what did they take from Burnt Island?
A coracle and paddle

B: In *The Voyage of the* Dawn Treader, who was the first mate?
Rhince

U: In *The Voyage of the* Dawn Treader, where did Lucy sleep?
In Caspian's cabin

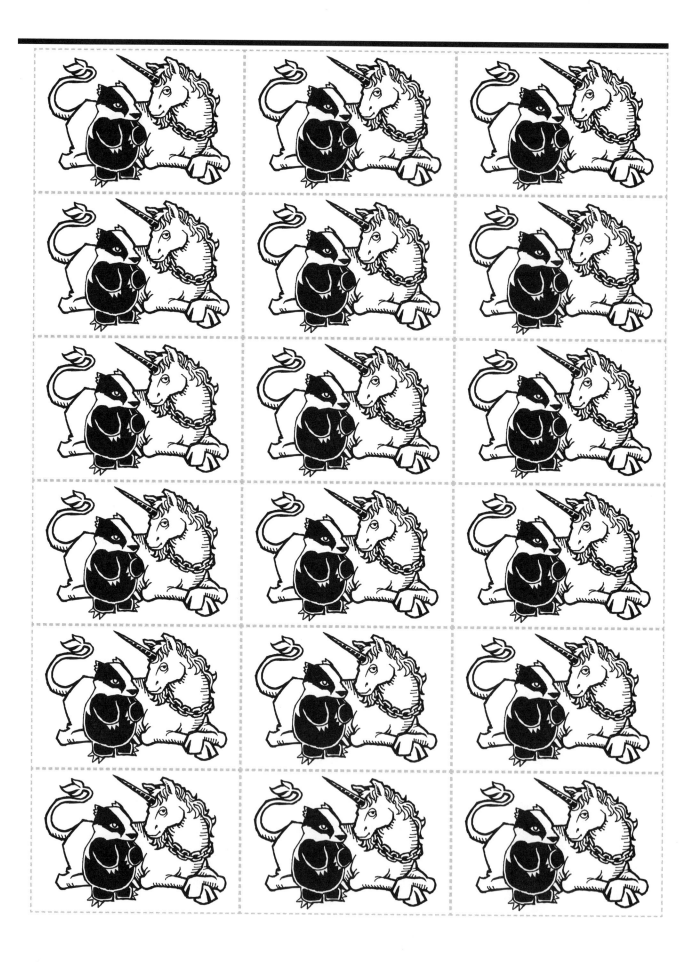

B: In *The Voyage of the* Dawn Treader, what did Coriakin make for them?
Maps

U: In *The Voyage of the* Dawn Treader, what crime was Lucy accused of magically committing?
Eavesdropping

B: In *The Voyage of the* Dawn Treader, what was unique about the Duffers?
They had only one foot

U: In *The Voyage of the* Dawn Treader, what effect did invisibility have on Coriakin?
It made him sleepy

B: In *The Voyage of the* Dawn Treader, what did Reepicheep suggest to the Monopods?
That they use their feet like boats

U: In *The Voyage of the* Dawn Treader, what did Lucy do on Dark Island?
She called on Aslan for help

B: In *The Voyage of the* Dawn Treader, what leads them away from Dark Island?
An albatross

U: In *The Voyage of the* Dawn Treader, what was the sacred relic kept on World's End island?
The Knife of Stone

B: In *The Voyage of the* Dawn Treader, whom did they find on Dark Island?
Lord Rhoop

U: In *The Voyage of the* Dawn Treader, what did Ramandu do before he lived on World's End?
He was a star

B: In *The Voyage of the* Dawn Treader, whom did they meet when they reached the end of the world?
Aslan

U: In *The Voyage of the* Dawn Treader, what did Ramandu receive each day?
A fire berry

B: In *The Voyage of the* Dawn Treader, what happened to Reepicheep the Mouse in the end?
He floated into Aslan's country

U: In *The Voyage of the* Dawn Treader, what did Ramandu give to Lord Rhoop?
Dreamless sleep

B: In *The Voyage of the* Dawn Treader, what happened to Ramandu's daughter in the end?
She married Caspian

U: In *The Voyage of the* Dawn Treader, what made the Silver Sea "silver?"
Lilies

B: In *The Silver Chair*, what terrifying thing happened to Eustace in Aslan's Country?
He fell over the cliff

U: In *The Silver Chair*, why was Jill Pole crying behind the gym?
She had been the recipient of bullying

B: In *The Silver Chair*, how did Jill travel to Narnia?
On the breath of Aslan

U: In *The Silver Chair*, what was the tale the blind bard told after their supper?
The Horse and his Boy

B: In *The Silver Chair*, how did Eustace travel to Narnia?
On the breath of Aslan

U: In *The Silver Chair*, how did the children muff the first Sign?
Eustace did not talk with his old friend the King

B: In *The Silver Chair*, what was the name of the King who sailed away from Narnia?
Caspian the Tenth, the Seafarer

U: In *The Silver Chair*, who was the only one to see Eustace and Jill fly into Narnia?
Glimfeather the Owl

B: In *The Silver Chair*, what happened to the mother of Rilian?
She was bitten by a green serpent during a nap

U: In *The Silver Chair*, what did the Warden say about those who go down into the Dark Realm?
Few return to the sunlit lands.

B: In *The Silver Chair*, who visited Jill in her dream at Harfang?
Aslan

U: In *The Silver Chair*, who was the first to greet the three travellers under the City Ruinous?
The Warden of the Marches of Underland

B: In *The Silver Chair*, what was the first thing Rilian did once he was free?
He destroyed the Silver Chair

U: In *The Silver Chair*, who was the enormous, sleeping, bearded man wrapped in silver light?
Father Time

B: In *The Silver Chair*, how did they kill the Queen?
They hacked off her head

U: In *The Silver Chair*, what happened to Rilian's black shield?
It had changed from black to silver with a red lion across it

B: In *The Silver Chair*, what was the name of the Really Deep Land?
The Land of Bism

U: In *The Silver Chair*, what did Puddleglum point out as the good thing about being trapped underground?
It saved on funeral expenses

B: In *The Silver Chair*, what task did Aslan set before Jill?
To seek the lost Narnian prince

U: In *The Silver Chair*, what were the fauns and dryads involved in when Jill's head popped up through the ground?
The Great Snow Dance

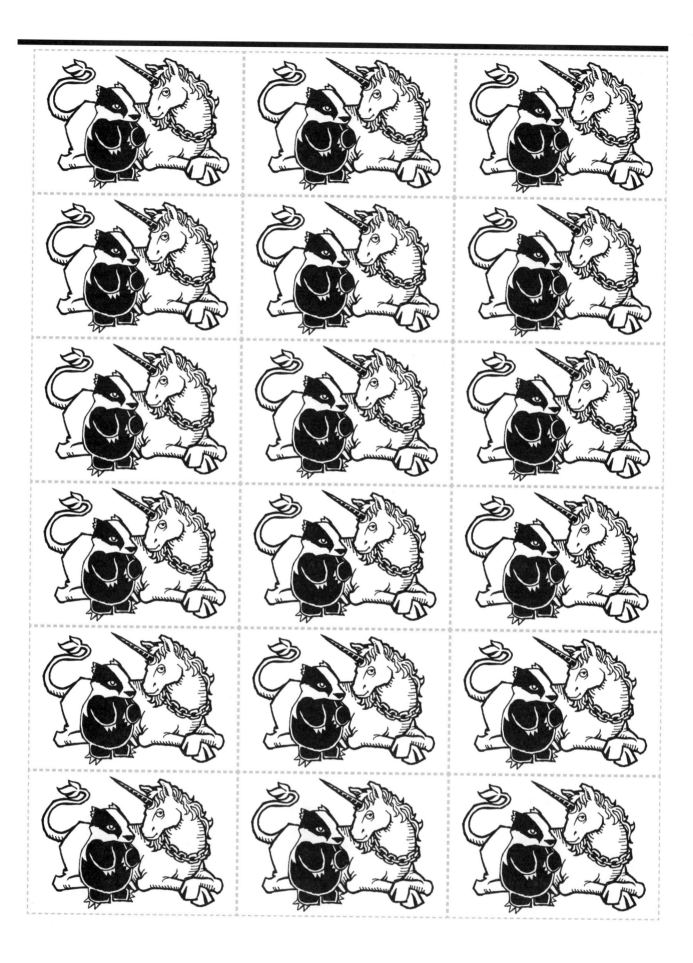

B: In *The Silver Chair*, who briefly went back to our world with Eustace and Jill?
Caspian

U: In *The Silver Chair*, how did Jill use her Narnian clothes in our world?
She wore them to a fancy dress ball

B: In *The Last Battle*, what was the only talking animal which listened to all the lies of the Ape calmly?
The cat, Ginger

U: In *The Last Battle*, what did Shift say was wrong with Narnia?
A lack of oranges, bananas and sugar

B: In *The Last Battle*, where did Shift live?
By Caldron Pool

U: In *The Last Battle*, what did Puzzle fish out of Caldron Pool?
A lion's skin

B: In *The Last Battle*, what kind of creature was Jewel?
Unicorn

U: In *The Last Battle*, what rash act did the Unicorn commit?
Gored a Calormen

B: In *The Last Battle*, who spoke to Tirian in a dream?
Peter the High King

U: In *The Last Battle*, what was the name of Narnia's North Star?
Spear-Head

B: In *The Last Battle*, what rash act did the King commit?
Beheaded a Calormen

U: In *The Last Battle*, what bad news did Roonwit bring?
Stories of Aslan being in Narnia was a lie

B: In *The Last Battle*, what was the name of the evil Ape?
Shift

U: In *The Last Battle*, what heretical statement about Aslan did Shift make?
Tash is Aslan: Aslan is Tash

B: In Narnian history, when did *The Horse and His Boy* take place?
The Golden Age—the reign of Peter, Edmund, Susan and Lucy

U: In *The Last Battle*, who retrieved the magic yellow and green rings?
Peter and Edmund

B: Who wrote *The Chronicles of Narnia?*
C.S. Lewis

U: Over what land did Swanwhite rule as Queen?
Narnia

B:

U:

B:

U:

B:

U:

B:

U:

B:

U:

B:

U:

B:

U:

B:

U:

B:

U:

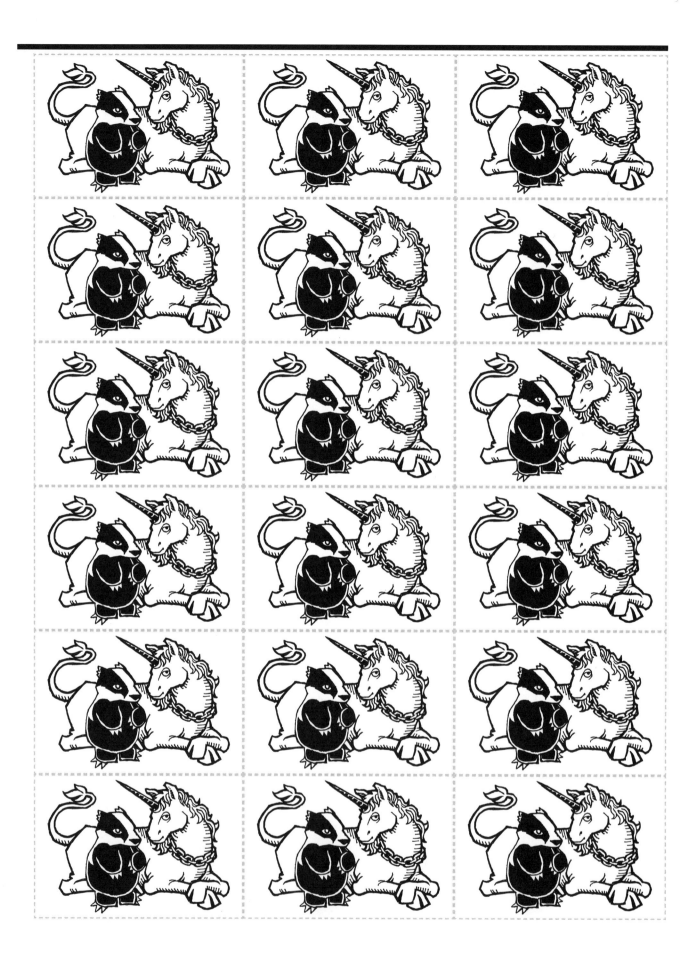

THE LAST BATTLE
The Badger and the Unicorn *Trivia Game*

Gameplay continued

If there is a tie for the highest bid, each of the players/teams who tied roll the die. The highest roll wins the right to answer the question. (In the event of a tied die roll, roll again as often as necessary to determine a winner.)

Whether or not the player/team that won the bid answers the question correctly, the auction counters used in the bid are then divided as evenly as possible among the remaining players/teams. Any leftover counters are placed in the middle of the table and will be divided among the players after the next auction is complete.

EXAMPLE: Anna wins the bid, bidding 5 auction counters. The other players are Brian, Charlie and Danielle. Brian, Charlie and Danielle would each receive one of Anna's 5 auction counters. The other two would be placed in the middle of the table to be divided after the next auction.

Repeat this process until all of the cards have been used. (Only one question from each card should be asked in this game. For example, if four players are playing, a total of 28 questions will be asked.)

At the end of the game, the player/team with the most points is the winner. If there is a tie, the players/teams who are tied for the lead ask each other difficult questions in sudden-death style to determine the winner.

THE LAST BATTLE
Chapter 9—"The Great Meeting on Stable Hill"

1. What did Jewel state was the obvious course of action, now that "Narnia is no more?"

   _____

   _____

   _____

   _____

2. Where did the King wish for the children to go, in light of this new plan?

   _____

   _____

   _____

   _____

3. What flaw in the King's wish did Eustace matter-of-factly point out?

   _____

   _____

   _____

   _____

4. What kind of death in England did Eustace say as worse than dying for Narnia?

   _____

   _____

   _____

   _____

5. How did the memory of King Miraz give the Narnians hope against the Calormen?

_____

_____

_____

_____

_____

6. What half-truth about "Tashlan" did Shift say at the bonfire that night which took the wind out of the sails of Jewel's plan?

_____

_____

_____

THE LAST BATTLE
Chapter 10—"Who Will Go Into the Stable?"

1. Following the cunning speech of the Ape, what did Jewel whisper to Jill that she should do?

   _____

   _____

   _____

2. What did Shift say to the Dwarfs who insisted on seeing what was in the stable?

   _____

   _____

   _____

3. The beasts were excited initially at the offer given by the Ape. What was it that Shift said which made them change their minds?

   _____

   _____

   _____

   _____

4. What did the King say to Jill to emcourage her when she voiced her fear of the possibility of Tash being in the stable?

   _____

   _____

   _____

5. What animal ended up going into the stable first?

   _____

   _____

6. What happened to this beast just before it disappeared up a tree, never to be seen again?

_____

_____

_____

7. Of who's blood did Rishda Tarkaan next declare himself guiltless?

_____

_____

8. What did the Calormen begin to do that thrust Tirian into action?

_____

_____

_____

THE LAST BATTLE
Chapter 11—"The Pace Quickens"

1. List the first three things which occurred once Tirian declared a call-to-arms to the Narnians.

   _____

   _____

   _____

   _____

   _____

2. Why did so few of the animals run to the King's side?

   _____

   _____

   _____

3. To what job did Tirian set the "nibblers, gnawers and nutcrackers?"

   _____

   _____

   _____

4. Who did Jill kill in the first melee with the Calormen's forces?

   _____

   _____

   _____

5. Why did the Dwarfs not come to the aid of the King?

   _____

   _____

   _____

6. What treachery befell the King's reinforcements?

_____

_____

_____

7. What did he hear that made the King give up all hope?

_____

_____

_____

8. What made the Calormen unprepared for Tirian's next attack?

_____

_____

_____

THE LAST BATTLE
Chapter 12—"Through the Stable Door"

1. Who of the King's band was captured and put into the stable as they retreated?

   _____

   _____

2. What did Rishda Tarkaan do to the Dwarfs he captured?

   _____

   _____

   _____

3. What ultimatum did the Tarkaan call out, an offer which was answered only by growls?

   _____

   _____

   _____

   _____

4. What weapon did the Calormen army possess which made the last battle of the last King of Narnia so hopeless?

   _____

   _____

5. What was the final deed Tirian did in Narnia?

   _____

   _____

6. What happened to Tash the Inexorable after it pounced on its "lawful prey?"

   _____

   _____

   _____

THE LAST BATTLE
Chapter 12, Page 2

7. What happened to Tirian's battle-worn appearance in the stable?

_____

_____

8. Who introduced the King to the High King?

_____

_____

9. What did High King Peter say when asked about Queen Susan the Gentle?

_____

_____

_____

_____

_____

THE LAST BATTLE
Chapter 13—"How the Dwarfs Refuse to Be Taken In"

1. What did they all do before Peter told them about how they had got into that land?

_____

_____

_____

2. Why had the Pevensie's parents been on the same train as Eustace and Jill?

_____

_____

3. How was the feeling of leaving England different for Lord Digory and Lady Polly than for the children?

_____

_____

_____

4. How did Queen Lucy compare the stable to a stable in our world?

_____

_____

_____

5. What did Queen Lucy reveal about what had happened to Ginger the Cat?

_____

_____

6. What did Diggle the Dwarf think the wild violets were which Lucy offered to him?

_____

_____

_____

7. What did Aslan give the Dwarfs to prove that they were no longer in the stable?

_____

_____

8. What set the Dwarfs to fighting one another?

_____

_____

_____

_____

THE LAST BATTLE
Chapter 14—"Night Falls on Narnia"

1. Where had Scrubb and Pole seen Time before Aslan woke him?

   _____

   _____

   _____

2. What was the immediate result of the giant blowing his horn?

   _____

   _____

   _____

3. Describe the appearance of this host of beings which assembled behind (and to the right of) Aslan, the kings and the queens.

   _____

   _____

   _____

   _____

   _____

4. What happened to the Talking Animals who looked into the face of Aslan with fear and hatred?

   _____

   _____

   _____

5. What "great joy" put wondering about the renegade Dwarf being allowed in through the doorway out of Eustace's mind?

   _____

   _____

   _____

6. What did Roonwit cry before thundering away into the West?

_____

_____

_____

7. What destroyed the vegetation in Narnia?

_____

_____

_____

8. What task did Aslan give to the High King after Time squeezed out the Sun?

_____

_____

_____

_____

9. What did the dogs sniff out?

_____

_____

THE LAST BATTLE
Chapter 15—"Further Up and Further In"

1. Why did Emeth's joy at marching against Narnia leave him?

   _____

   _____

2. Why did Aslan take Emeth's service to Tash as service to the Lion?

   _____

   _____

3. At what Calormen figure of speech did the Talking Dogs take offense?

   _____

   _____

4. What did Farsight realize about the land through which they walked?

   _____

   _____

5. What did Lord Digory say which caused the older children to laugh?

   _____

   _____

6. What did they all learn about themselves when Jewel sprang forward into a great gallop?

   _____

   _____

   _____

THE LAST BATTLE
Chapter 16—"Farewell to Shadowlands"

1. What briefly stopped their progress at the edge of the real Narnia?

   _____

   _____

   _____

2. Who were the only ones of the company to recognize the lands of the Western Wild? Why?

   _____

   _____

   _____

3. Who greeted them when the golden gates of the garden opened?

   _____

   _____

4. What creature perched above King Frank and Queen Helen in the center of the orchard?

   _____

   _____

5. According to Mr. Tumnus, how was the real Narnia *unlike* an onion?

_____

_____

_____

6. What did the children discover had not been destroyed in the real England?

_____

_____

_____

7. What did Aslan tell them happened in the Shadowlands, which meant they would never have to leave Aslan's Country, but that instead, "The term is over: the holidays have begun?"

_____

_____

_____

_____

THE LAST BATTLE
Project—Recurring Themes

C.S. Lewis throughout the Chronicles visits and revisits themes to communicate aspects of Narnia's uniqueness or the tactile nature of things so the reader can experience the magic more fully. Write an essay drawing from all seven books to describe how one of the following elements are used: Food, Beauty, Doors, Music, Water. *This project is best done by fifth graders and above.*

THE CHRONICLES OF NARNIA
Reference to Names

Following is a quick reference guide for the Chronicles. For an excellent, exhaustive and expert reference to all things Narnian, consult Paul F. Ford's Companion to Narnia

A

Adela Pennyfather:	A student at Experiment House [SC]
Ahoshta Tarkaan:	The Calormene Grand Vizier betrothed to Aravis [HHB]
Alambil:	A Narnian star also known as "Lady of Peace" [PC]
Alberta Scrubb:	Eustace Scrubb's mother [VDT]
Alimash:	Aravis' cousin, and captain of the chariots in the Calormene army [HHB]
Andrew Ketterly:	Digory Kirke's uncle who crafted magic rings [MN]
Anne Featherstone:	One of Lucy's schoolmates [VDT]
Anradin:	A Calormene Tarkaan and owner of Bree [HHB]
Anvard:	The castle of Archenland
Aravis:	A Tarkheena who befriended the horse Hwin and mother of Ram the Great [HHB]
Archenland:	The country south of Narnia, bordered to the south by the Great Desert
Ardeeb Tisroc:	The great-great-great-grandfather of Aravis [HHB]
Argoz:	One of the seven lost lords [PC] [VDT]
Arlian:	A Narnian lord under Caspian IX that was executed for treason on a false charge [PC]
Arsheesh:	A poor Calormene fisherman who takes in the infant Shasta [HHB]
Aslan:	The Great Lion, the son of the Emperor-over-the-sea, the king above all high kings in Narnia [MN] [LWW] [HHB] [PC] [VDT] [SC] [LB]
Aslan's How:	The mound raised over the Stone Table [PC]
Aslan's Table:	A table on Ramandu's Island where a constant feast is laid out and where the Stone Knife is kept [VDT]
Avra:	The easternmost of the Lone Islands

Axartha:	A Grand Vizier of Calormen before Ahoshta [HHB]
Azaroth:	A Calormene goddess [HHB]
Azim Balda:	A Calormene city southwest of Tasbaan [HHB]

B

Bacchus:	The Roman god of wine [LWW] [PC]
Bar:	An embezzling lord chancellor from Archenland [HHB]
Battle of Beruna:	The Battle between Caspian X's and Miraz's forces [PC]
Beaversdam:	A town in Narnia, located at the place where Mr. and Mrs. Beaver's home was situated [PC]
Belisar:	A Narnian lord under Caspian IX who was shot while he was with a hunting party [PC]
Bern:	One of the seven lost lords and Duke of the Lone Islands [PC] [VDT]
Bernstead:	A town on the island of Avra in the Lone Islands [VDT]
Beruna:	A Narnian town located on the River Rush [PC]
Beruna Bridge:	A bridge built in Beruna by the Telmarines of Narnia [PC]
Betty:	One of Professor Kirke's servants [LWW]
Big Bannister:	A student at Experiment House [SC]
Bism:	A land of gnomes and fire salamanders deep under the earth [SC]
Black Woods:	The term used by the Telmarines of Narnia to describe the forest in eastern Narnia [PC]
Bree:	A horse that helps Shasta escape Calormen [HHB]
Brenn:	One of the islands that makes up the Seven Isles [VDT]
Bricklethumb:	A Dwarf of Narnia; brother to Rogin and Duffle [HHB]
Buffins:	A respectable family of Narnian giants [LWW]
Bulgy Bears:	Three Talking Bears of Old Narnia [PC]
Burnt Island:	An uninhabited island near Dragon Island [VDT]

THE CHRONICLES OF NARNIA
Reference to Names

C

Cair Paravel: The castle where all true kings and queens of Narnia rule [LWW] [HHB] [PC] [VDT] [SC] [LB]

Calavar: A Calormene province [HHB]

Calormen: Barbaric land south of Narnia and Archenland [LWW] [HHB] [PC] [VDT] [SC] [LB]

Camillo: A Talking Hare of Old Narnia [PC]

Caspian I: Caspian the Conqueror; Telmarine who conquered Old Narnia [PC]

Caspian IX: Father of Caspian X; his throne was usurped by his brother Miraz [PC]

Caspian X: Caspian the Seafarer, hero of the War of Deliverance, father of Rilian the Disenchanted [VDT] [SC]

Cauldron Pool: The big pool right under the cliffs at the western end of Narnia [LB]

Charn: The original home of Jadis [MN]

Chervy: A Talking Stag of Narnia [HHB]

Chief of the messengers: The Dispatcher of Messages at Azim Balda in Calormen [HHB]

Chippingford: A Narnian town [LB]

City Ruinous: The ruined giant city in the northern wastelands [SC]

Clipsie: The daughter of the chief Dufflepud [VDT]

Clodsley Shovel: The chief of the Talking Moles of Narnia [PC]

Cloudbirth: A famous healer Centaur [SC]

Coalblack: Prince Rilian's horse [SC]

Cole: A lord of Archenland (Brother of Colin) [HHB]

Colin: A lord of Archenland (Brother of Cole) [HHB]

Cor: Eldest son of King Lune, savior of Archenland and father of Ram the Great [HHB]

Coriakin: A fallen star given charge of the Dufflepuds [VDT]

Corin: Cor's brother; becomes known as Corin Thunder-fist of Archenland [HHB] [LB]

Corradin of Castle Tormunt: A Tarkaan of Rabadash's army [HHB]

D

Dancing Lawn: A circle of grass used for dancing by the Fauns of Old Narnia while in hiding; used by Caspian X for a council of war [PC]

Dar: A lord of Archenland [HHB]

Darrin: A lord of Archenland [HHB]

Dawn Treader: Caspian X's ship [VDT]

Deathwater Island: An island that has a lake that turns things into gold [VDT]

Deep Realm: Part of Underland [SC]

Destrier: Caspian X's horse [PC]

Diggle: A bad dwarf [LB]

Digory Kirke: Son of Mabel Kirke, and one of the first to visit Narnia [MN] [LWW] [LB]

Doorn: Largest of the Lone Islands [VDT]

Dr. Cornelius: Caspian X's half-dwarf tutor [PC]

Dragon Island: An uninhabited island [VDT]

Drinian: Captain of the Dawn Treader [VDT]

Duffle: A red dwarf of Narnia; brother of Rogin and Bricklethumb [HHB]

Dufflepuds: A race of dwarves that have only one foot each [VDT]

Dumnus: A faun of Old Narnia [PC]

E

Earlian: Second-to-last king of Narnia, and father of Tirian [LB]

Eastern Ocean: The ocean east of Narnia [MN] [LWW] [HHB] [PC] [VDT] [SC] [LB]

Edmund Pevensie: The second youngest of the Pevensies, Edmund becomes known as King Edmund the Just [LWW] [HHB] [PC] [VDT] [LB]

Emeth: A noble young Calormene who finds the truth [LB]

Erimon: Narnian lord under Caspian IX; Erimon was executed for treason on a false charge [PC]

Ettinsmoor: The rocky plains north of Narnia that are inhabited by giants, also called "Ettinsmuir" [SC] [LB]

Eustace Clarence Scrubb: A cousin of the Pevensies who helped free Prince Rilian [VDT] [SC] [LB]

Experiment House: The school that Eustace and Jill attend [SC]

THE CHRONICLES OF NARNIA
Reference to Names

F

Fair Olvin: He fought the giant Pire [HHB]

Far Sight: A Talking Eagle [LB]

Father Christmas: Saint Nicholas [LWW]

Father Time: The giant sleeping beneath the earth [SC] [LB]

Felimath: Northernmost of the Lone Islands [VDT]

Felinda: A ruined city mentioned by Jadis [MN]

Fenris Ulf: A gray wolf, captain of the White Witch's secret police (also called Maugrim) [LWW]

Flaming Mountain of Lagour: A Calormene volcano [LB]

Fledge: The first winged horse of Narnia, formerly known as Strawberry [MN]

Fords of Beruna: Fords in the River Rush, located at the town of Beruna [PC]

Frank I: A cabby in London and Narnia's first king [MN]

H

Hall of Images: The hall in Charn [MN]

Harfang: House of the "Gentle Giants," north of Narnia [SC]

Harold Scrubb: Eustace Scrubb's father [VDT]

Harpa Tarkaan: A Calormen, the father of Emeth [LB]

Helen: Wife of Frank I; also called "Nellie" [MN] [LB]

Hermit of the Southern March: A kind old Hermit of Archenland [HHB]

Hogglestock: A Talking Hedgehog of Old Narnia [PC]

House of Imperial Posts: The place from which posts are sent at Azim Balda [HHB]

Hwin: A horse that helps Aravis escape Calormen [HHB]

I

Ilkeen: A Calormene area where a lake is located [HHB]

Ilsambreh Tisroc: The great-great-grandfather of Aravis Tarkheena [HHB]

Ivy: A servant of Professor Kirke's [LWW]

J

Jadis: The last queen of Charn [MN] [LWW]

Jewel: A unicorn, and one of King Tirian's closest friends [LB]

Jill Pole: A friend of Eustace who helped free Prince Rilian [SC] [LB]

K

Kidrash Tarkaan: The names of Aravis' father and great-grandfather [HHB]

Knife of Stone: The knife the White Witch used for ritual sacrifices [LWW] [VDT]

L

Lady Liln: The wife of Fair Olvin [HHB]

Lady of the Green Kirtle: A Northern witch [SC]

Lantern Waste: The forest around the Lamp Post in Western Narnia [MN] [LWW] [HHB] [PC] [SC] [LB]

Lapsed Bear of Stormness: A Talking Bear that had gone back to wild bear habits [HHB]

Lasaraleen Tarkheena: A friend of Aravis Tarkheena [HHB]

Letitia Ketterly: Digory's aunt [MN]

Lilith: According to Hebrew tradition, she was Adam's first wife. She left Adam before the Fall and thus escaped the curse of death. [LWW]

Lilygloves: Head of the Talking Moles during the Golden Age of Narnia [PC]

Lone Islands: Islands belonging to Narnia, located far out in the ocean [VDT] [LB]

Lucy Pevensie: The youngest Pevensie child who becomes Queen Lucy the Valiant [LWW] [HHB] [PC] [VDT] [LB]

Lune: A good king of Archenland, father of Cor and Corin [HHB]

THE CHRONICLES OF NARNIA
Reference to Names

M

Mabel Kirke: Digory's mother [MN]
Maenads: Bacchus' "mad-cap" girls [PC]
Margaret: A servant of Professor Kirke [LWW]
Marjorie Preston: One of Lucy's schoolmates [VDT]
Mavramorn: One of the seven lost lords [PC] [VDT]
Mentius: A faun of Old Narnia [PC]
Mezreel: A lake in Calormen [HHB]
Miraz: Uncle of Caspian X, and usurper of the Narnian throne [PC]
Miss Prizzle: A teacher at a girl's school in Beruna [PC]
Moonwood: A Talking Hare who had such ears that he could sit by Caldron Pool and hear what was said in whispers at Cair Paravel [LB]
Mount Pire: A double-headed mountain in Archenland, which was once a living giant [HHB]
Mr. & Mrs. Beaver: Two beavers that helped the Pevensies [LWW]
Mrs. Lefay: Uncle Andrew's godmother [MN]
Mrs. Macready: Professor Kirke's housekeeper [LWW]
Muil: The westernmost of the Seven Isles [VDT]
Mulugutherum: The Warden of the Marches of Underland [SC]

N

Nain: King of Archenland during Miraz's reign [PC]
Narnia: The land that lies between the Lamp Post in the west and Cair Paravel in the east [MN] [LWW] [HHB] [PC] [VDT] [SC] [LB]
Narrowhaven: A town on the island of Doorn in the Lone Islands [VDT]
Nausus: A faun of Old Narnia [PC]
Nikabrik: A black dwarf of Old Narnia [PC]
Nimienus: A faun of Old Narnia [PC]

O

Obentinus: A faun of Old Narnia [PC]
Octesian: One of the seven lost lords [PC] [VDT]
Orruns: A faun [SC]
Oscuns: A faun of Old Narnia [PC]

P

Passarids: A great Narnian house during Caspian IX's reign who were killed fighting giants [PC]
Pattertwig: A Talking Squirrel [PC]
Peepiceek: Head of the Talking Mice after Reepicheep [PC] [VDT]
Peridan: A Narnian lord [HHB]
Peter Pevensie: High King of Narnia, and oldest of the Pevensie children who was also called 'King Peter the Magnificent' [LWW] [HHB] [PC] [LB]
Pittencream: A sailor on the Dawn Treader who didn't sail on to the end of the world, but stayed on Ramandu's Island [VDT]
Poggin: A good Dwarf [LB]
Polly Plummer: Digory's neighbor and one of the first to visit Narnia [MN] [LB]
Pomely: Glozelle's horse [PC]
Prunaprismia: Miraz's wife [PC]
Puddleglum: A valiant Marshwiggle who helped free Prince Rilian [SC]
Pug: A leader of the slave trade in the Lone Islands [VDT]
Pugrahan: Salt pits in Calormen [LB]
Puzzle: A simple donkey used to deceive Narnia [LB]

THE CHRONICLES OF NARNIA
Reference to Names

R

Rabadash:	A Calormene prince who tries to get Queen Susan to marry him [HHB]
Ram the Great:	Son of Cor and Aravis, and greatest of all the kings of Archenland [HHB]
Ramandu:	An old star sent to an island to grow young and grandfather to Prince Rilian [VDT]
Ramandu's Island:	The home of the star Ramandu that has also been called World's End, Island of the Star and Island of the Three Sleepers [VDT]
Raven of Ravenscaur:	A Talking Raven [PC]
Redhaven:	A city in the Seven Isles, located on the island called Brenn [VDT]
Reepicheep:	Head of the Talking Mice who sailed beyond the end of the world [PC] [VDT] [LB]
Restimar:	One of the seven lost lords [PC] [VDT]
Revilian:	One of the seven lost lords [PC] [VDT]
Rhince:	First mate on the Dawn Treader [VDT]
Rhindon:	Peter's sword [PC]
Rhoop:	One of the seven lost lords [PC] [VDT]
Rilian:	Son of Caspian X, called "Rilian the Disenchanted" [SC] [LB]
Rishda Tarkaan:	Head of the Calormenes infiltration into Narnia [LB]
Rishti Tarkaan:	Aravis' grandfather [HHB]
Rogin:	A Dwarf of Narnia; brother to Bricklethumb and Duffle [HHB]
Roonwit:	A faithful Centaur [LB]
Rumblebuffin:	A good Giant [LWW]
Rush:	A river in southern Narnia [PC]
Rynelf:	A sailor aboard the Dawn Treader [VDT]

S

Sallowpad:	A Talking Raven [HHB]
Sarah:	The Ketterley's housemaid [MN]
Seven Brothers of Shuddering Wood:	Seven Dwarves of Old Narnia that run a smithy [PC]
Seven Isles:	Seven islands that are part of Narnia [PC] [VDT]
Shar:	A lord of Archenland [HHB]
Shasta:	Adopted son of a Calormene fisherman who runs away to Archenland [HHB]
Shift:	A wicked Ape [LB]
Shribble:	The river separating Narnia from Ettinsmoor [SC]
Silenus:	In Greek mythology, Silenus was the teacher of Dionysus who rode a donkey [PC]
Silver Sea:	The last sea before Aslan's Country [VDT]
Slinky:	A fox who betrays Narnia [LB]
Snowflake:	The Lady of the Green Kirtle's horse [SC]
Sopespian:	A lord in Miraz's army [PC]
Sorlois:	A ruined city mentioned by Jadis [MN]
Spear Head:	The Narnian north star [PC]
Splendor Hyaline:	The ship of King Edmund, King Peter, Queen Susan, and Queen Lucy [HHB]
Stable Hill:	The name of the hill where the lie starts [LB]
Stonefoot:	A good Giant [LB]
Stone Table:	An ancient table of stone [LWW] [PC]
Stormness Head:	A mountain on the border of Narnia and Archenland [HHB]
Strawberry:	The cabby's horse, later known as Fledge [MN]
Susan Pevensie:	Second oldest Pevensie child, she becomes Queen Susan the Gentle [LWW] [HHB] [PC] [LB]
Swanwhite:	A beautiful queen of Narnia [LB]

T

Tarva:	A Narnian star, also known as the "Lord of Victory" [PC]
Tash:	The main god of the Calormenes [HHB] [LB]
Tashbaan:	The capital city of Calormen, located on an island in a river [HHB]
Teebeth:	A Calormen province taken in battle [HHB]
Tehishbaan:	A city in Calormen [LB]
Telmar:	A wild land far to the west of Narnia [PC]
Terebinthia:	An island off the coast of Narnia [VDT]
Thornbut:	The Dwarf ordered to watch over Corin at the war against the Calormenes [HHB]
Three Hardbiters:	Three Talking Badgers of Old Narnia [PC]
Tirian:	The last king of Narnia [LB]
Tisroc:	Term for the ruler of Calormen [HHB] [LB]
Tombs of the Ancient Kings:	Giant bee-hive shaped tombs located at the edge of the Great Desert [HHB]
Tran:	A lord of Archenland [HHB]
Truffle-hunter:	A faithful badger [PC]
Trumpkin:	A good Dwarf and Lord Regent to King Caspian [PC] [VDT] [SC]
Tumnus:	A good faun that befriends Lucy [LWW] [HHB]

UV

Urnus:	A faun [SC]
Uvilas:	Narnian lord under Caspian IX who was shot while with a hunting party [PC]
Valley of the Thousand Perfumes:	A valley located near the lake Mezreel [HHB]
Voluns:	A faun of Old Narnia [PC]
Voltinus:	A faun of Old Narnia [PC]

WXYZ

Western Wilds:	The woods west of Narnia [MN] [PC]
Winding Arrow:	A river in southern Archenland [HHB]
White Stag:	A stag said to grant wishes to whomever catches it [LWW]
White Witch:	Jadis, Last of Charn who ruled Narnia for 100 years, making it winter all the time [MN] [LWW]
Wimbleweather:	A good (but slow) Giant [PC]
Wood Between the Worlds:	A crossroads between all worlds [MN]
Wraggle:	A satyr who betrays Narnia [LB]
Zardeenah:	Lady of the Night and Maidens— a Calormene goddess [HHB]
Zulindreh:	A Calormene location where a battle took place [HHB]

THE CHRONICLES OF NARNIA
Narnian/English Timelines

NARNIA	ENGLAND

NARNIA

Year:

1 — Creation of Narnia. The Beasts made able to talk. Digory plants the Tree of Protection. The White Witch Jadis enters Narnia but flies into the far North. Frank I becomes King of Narnia.

180 — Prince Col, younger son of King Frank V of Narnia leads certain followers into Archenland (not then inhabited) and becomes first king of that country.

204 — Certain outlaws from Archenland fly across the southern desert and set up the new kingdom of Calormen.

300 — The empire of Calormen spreads mightily. Calormenes colonize the land of Telmar to the west of Narnia.

302 — The Calormenes in Telmar behave very wickedly and Aslan turns them into dumb beasts. The country lies waste. King Gale of Narnia delivers the Lone Islands from a dragon and is made emperor by their grateful inhabitants.

407 — Olvin of Archenland kills the Giant Pire.

460 — Pirates from our world take possession of Telmar.

570 — About this time lived Moonwood the Hare.

898 — The White Witch Jadis returns into Narnia out of the far North.

900 — The long winter begins.

1000 — The Pevensies arrive in Narnia. The treachery of Edmund. The sacrifice of Aslan. The White Witch defeated and the Long Winter ended. Peter becomes High King of Narnia.

ENGLAND

Year:

1888 — Digory Kirke born.

1889 — Polly Plummer born.

1900 — Polly and Digory carried into Narnia by magic rings.

1927 — Peter Pevensie born.

1928 — Susan Pevensie born.

1930 — Edmund Pevensie born.

1932 — Lucy Pevensie born.

1933 — Eustace Scrubb and Jill Pole born.

1940 — The Pevensies, staying with Digory (now Professor) Kirke, reach Narnia through the Magic Wardrobe.

NARNIA	ENGLAND
Year:	**Year:**
1014 — King Peter carries out a successful raid on the Northern Giants. Queen Susan and King Edmund visit the Court of Calormen. King Lune of Archenland discovers his long-lost son Prince Cor and defeats a treacherous attack by Prince Rabadash of Calormen.	
1015 — The Pevensies hunt the White Stag and vanish out of Narnia.	1940 — The Pevensies leave Narnia through the Magic Wardrobe.
1050 — Ram the Great succeeds Cor as King of Archenland.	
1502 — About this time lived Queen Swanwhite of Narnia.	
1998 — The Telmarines invade and conquer Narnia. Caspian I becomes King of Narnia.	
2290 — Prince Caspian, son of Caspian IX, born. Caspian IX murdered by his brother Miraz who usurps the throne.	
2303 — Prince Caspian escapes from his uncle Miraz. By the aid of Aslan and of the Pevensies, whom Caspian summons with Queen Susan's Magic Horn, Miraz is defeated and killed during the War of Deliverance. Caspian becomes King Caspian X of Narnia.	1941 — The Pevensies again caught into Narnia by the blast of the Magic Horn.
2304 — Caspian X defeats the Northern Giants.	
2306-7 — Caspian X's great voyage to the end of the World.	1942 — Edmund, Lucy, and Eustace reach Narnia again and take part in Caspian's voyage.
2310 — Caspian X marries Ramandu's daughter.	
2325 — Prince Rilian born.	
2345 — The Queen killed by a Serpent. Rilian disappears.	
2356 — Eustace and Jill appear in Narnia and rescue Prince Rilian. Death of Caspian X	1942 — Eustace and Jill, from Experiment House, are carried away into Narnia.
2534 — Outbreak of outlaws in Lantern Waste. Towers built to guard that region.	
2555 — Rebellion of Shift the Ape. King Tirian rescued by Eustace and Jill. Narnia in the hands of the Calormenes. The last battle. End of the World.	1949 — Serious accident on British Railways.

THE CHRONICLES OF NARNIA
Answers

THE MAGICIAN'S NEPHEW
"The Wrong Door"
1. Sir Arthur Conan Doyle's Sherlock Holmes and the Bastables from E. Nesbit's book The Bastable Children.
2. Crying
3. A tunnel behind the row houses which they called the Cave
4. The empty "haunted" house beyond Digory's
5. A bright red wooden tray with yellow and green rings upon it
6. Tall and thin with a clean-shaven face, a sharp nose, bright eyes and a great tousled mop of grey hair
7. One of the humming yellow rings

"Digory and His Uncle"
1. Screams
2. Mrs. Lefay; Morgan Le Fay of Arthurian legend was a wicked sorceress
3. She had fairy blood in her
4. Atlantis
5. Uncle Andrew thought that rules concerning things that are right and wrong did not apply to his godmother or "profound students and great thinkers . . . [possessors] of hidden wisdom"—which was what he considered himself.
6. They only worked if they actually touched skin

"The Wood Between the Worlds"
1. A dreamy wooded place as rich as plum-cake. There were small pools of water among the tall trees and the sunlight that filtered through the dense leaves overhead was warm and green. It was completely quiet there and had a feeling of timelessness.
2. The guinea pig
3. The tunnel
4. They must know they could return to our world
5. That Digory mark the pool (he cut a strip from the turf with his pocket knife)
6. Yellow rings took you into the Woods and the green rings took you out of the woods into another world.

"The Bell and the Hammer"
1. It was a dull red light
2. It was silent
3. The faces changed from being those of nice people to cruel faces
4. A little golden arch from which hung a little golden bell with a little golden hammer laying beside it on top of a four foot high square pillar
5. He wished to strike the bell and she did not
6. He struck the bell

"The Deplorable Word"
1. It woke Queen Jadis
2. Dungeons, torture chambers and other infamous rooms
3. Using the Deplorable Word
4. Like Uncle Andrew, claiming to be free from all rules that "common" people must adhere to.
5. That Uncle Andrew was a great Magician king, ruler of our world, and that he sent Digory to fetch Jadis out his love for her beauty
6. In a rage, the Queen dropped the children's hands and grabbed Polly's hair (where it hurts the most)

"The Beginning of Uncle Andrew's Troubles"
1. Holding onto Polly's hair
2. It weakened her—she felt it was killing her
3. Giantish blood in the royal family of Charn
4. A flying carpet or a well-trained dragon
5. She would lay spells on him that feel like red hot iron if he sat down and invisible blocks of ice if he lay down
6. Twisting Polly's wrist, striking the bell, and letting the Queen follow from the Woods attached to Digory's ear
7. He dressed in his fanciest clothes then kept admiring himself in the mirror, congratulating himself on magically drawing the "dem fine woman" into our world. He also began to imagine that the Witch would fall in love with him
8. By borrowing money from his sister Aunt Letty

THE CHRONICLES OF NARNIA
Comprehension Question Answers

"What Happened at the Front Door"
1. The circus
2. Turn her into dust
3. Take her back to the Woods between the Worlds
4. Fruit from the Land of Youth
5. Standing on the roof of a hansom, teeth bared, flogging a horse mercilessly
6. A second hansom bearing a fat jeweler and a policeman, a third hansom bearing police, errand boys on bicycles, and a crowd of people on foot
7. The Cabby whose horse the Witch had stolen

"The Fight at the Lamp-Post"
1. Hempress of Colney 'Atch
2. One of the cross-bars of a lamp-post
3. The heel of Jadis
4. Jadis, Uncle Andrew, the Horse and the Cabby
5. He went to get a drink at one of the pools, and when he did, the children put on their green rings
6. Nothing
7. Sing a hymn
8. Get Digory to put on the ring and take him home
9. Stars
10. The singing represented a different, stronger Magic than hers
11. A huge, shaggy Lion

"The Founding of Narnia"
1. Stealing the rings
2. She robbed a jeweler and made Uncle Andrew provide her with an ostentatious lunch
3. She threw the cross-bar at the Lion
4. Shoot it with a gun
5. A lamp-post
6. The land of youth
7. They encircled the Lion then changed in size
8. Awake, love, think and speak. Be walking trees, talking beasts and divine waters

"The First Joke and Other Matters"
1. Fauns, satyrs, dwarfs, the river god and naiads
2. I give you yourselves, the land of Narnia, the woods, the fruits, the rivers, the stars and Aslan (the Turkish word for lion, pronounced "Ass-lan"). Care for the dumb animals but do not act like them or you'll become like them.
3. The Jackdaw
4. The chief Dwarf, the River-god, the Oak, the He-Owl, the Ravens and the Bull-Elephant

5. Sugar cubes
6. He willed himself to hear it only as a "horrid, bloodthirsty din of hungry and angry brutes"
7. Animal, vegetable, or mineral?

"Digory and His Uncle Are Both in Trouble"
1. Fainted
2. Money—two half-sovereigns, three half crowns and a sixpence
3. A tree
4. "Evil will come of this evil, but it is still a long way off, and I will see to it that the worst falls upon myself."
5. King and Queen in Narnia
6. "You shall rule and name all these creatures, and do justice among them, and protect them from their enemies when enemies arise."
7. If she had forgiven Digory

"Strawberry's Adventure"
1. Tears in the eyes of Aslan
2. That she would return to Narnia
3. A kiss
4. Past the great waterfall, through the Western Wild, up on the top of a steep green hill found by a blue lake ringed by mountains in the center of a garden
5. He didn't feel he deserved the honor, not being a clever horse
6. Toffee
7. The signs given to them by Aslan
8. According to Polly, a tall, dark figure gliding quickly to the West

"An Unexpected Meeting"
1. Fruit from a toffee tree
2. Branches from the trees within the garden hung over a high wall of green turf which had high golden gates inset, facing east
3. Come in by the gold gates or not at all,
Take of my fruit for others or forbear,
For those who steal, or those who climb my wall
Shall find their heart's desire and find despair.
4. Stealing an apple for himself
5. The Witch; eaten an apple; her skin became completely white
6. Knowledge that would make Digory happy for the rest of his life
7. It was the apple of youth, of life
8. She suggested leaving without Polly

THE CHRONICLES OF NARNIA
Comprehension Question Answers

9. The memory of the shining tears in the eyes of Aslan

"The Planting of the Tree"
1. Well Done
2. It was thrown into the mud along the river bank
3. Brandy
4. Sleep
5. The trees grown from Uncle Andrew's money that had fallen from his pockets
6. Narnia, the Isles and Archenland (pronounced, "Ar-K-enland")
7. The Tree of Protection
8. The smell of the tree
9. Pluck an apple from the Tree

"The End of This Story and the Beginning of all the Others"
1. The dry pool in the Wood between the Worlds which once led to Charn
2. The golden goodness of Aslan
3. No time at all
4. Get the other rings to bury as Aslan had commanded
5. She smiled and fell asleep
6. A tree was already growing up from the apple core Digory had planted
7. Old Great-Uncle Kirk's country house
8. King Frank's second son
9. It was made into a wardrobe

THE LION THE WITCH AND THE WARDROBE
"Lucy Looks into a Wardrobe"
1. World War II air raids over London
2. Peter, Susan, Edmund, Lucy
3. It was raining
4. A wardrobe
5. It is very foolish to shut oneself into a wardrobe
6. A lamppost in the woods
7. It was a Faun carrying an umbrella. Glossy black goats legs and tail. He had a short pointed beard and curly hair and two horns.

"What Lucy Found the There"
1. Daughter of Eve
2. Mr. Tumnus
3. From the lamppost to the great castle of Cair Paravel
4. Spare Oom

5. His cave
6. Wishes
7. White Witch
8. Always winter and never Christmas
9. Handkerchief

"Edmund and the Wardrobe"
1. No time had passed and the back of the wardrobe was solid
2. Hide and seek
3. To tease Lucy about her imaginary country
4. Two white reindeer
5. And fat dwarf dressed in polar bear's fur and a red hood. A tall woman covered in white fur, wearing a golden crown and carrying a long golden wand

"Turkish Delight"
1. Copper
2. A very sweet, foamy and creamy hot drink
3. Turkish Delight
4. Prince
5. White Witch
6. Between two hills

"Back on this Side of the Door"
1. He said Narnia didn't exist—he and Lucy were pretending
2. They thought Lucy was out of her mind
3. Logic
4. Lucy was telling lies / She was mad / She was telling the truth
5. The difference in the passing of time between our world and Narnia
6. It was old and famous, found in histories and guidebooks
7. Either they lost their heads, or Macready was trying to catch them, or magic in the house

"Into the Forest"
1. Fur coats
2. It was burned and ransacked, or a piece of paper nailed to the floor
3. Comforting the Queen's enemies / harboring spies / fraternizing with humans
4. Fenris Ulf or Maugrim

THE CHRONICLES OF NARNIA
Comprehension Question Answers

"A Day with the Beavers"
1. Lucy's handkerchief
2. Aslan
3. His dam/den
4. Sewing
5. Trout, bread and butter, boiled potatoes, beer, creamy milk, and marmalade roll for dessert
6. Bunkbeds built into walls, hams and onions hanging from the ceiling, table with three-legged stools, gum boots, oil skins, hatchets, shears, spades, trowels, fishing rods, nets and sacks

"What Happened after Dinner"
1. Taken to the Queen's house and possibly turned to stone
2. The Lion, King and Lord of the Wood, Son of the great Emperor-Beyond-the-Sea
3. Lilith and giants. In Hebrew myth God formed Lilith, the first woman, just as He had formed Adam, except that he used filth and sediment instead of pure dust. Their children were said to be the innumerable demons that still plague mankind. Lilith escaped the curse of death which overtook Adam, because they had parted long before the Fall. Lilith is said to strangle infants and seduce dreaming men.

   Though the beavers say that she is the daughter of Lilith and a Jinn, we know a different origin from *The Magician's Nephew*. This apparent inconsistancy might be explained within the *Chronicles* as Narnian folklore that arose among the Narnians during the Long Winter. Centuries of peace in Narnia would doubtless have lulled the Narnians into a forgetfulness about the "Neevil." So when Jadis returned, they may have had vague recollection of of the events at the Creation of their world, but would have had no histories of what transpired before chapter nine in *The Magician's Nephew*. But the king of Narnia who was defeated when Jadis took over Narnia would surely have had bedtime stories passed down about Lilith and the jinn from their royal great-great-great-grandparents King Frank and Queen Helen.
4. Two sons of Adam and two daughters of Eve sat on the four thrones of Cair Paravel or
   When Adam's flesh and Adam's bone
   Sits at Cair Paravel in throne,
   The evil time will be over and done.
5. His eyes
6. Edmund leaving

"In the Witch's House"
1. Fur coat
2. Make some decent roads
3. Lion
4. Aslan
5. Scribbled a mustache on him
6. Fenris Ulf or Maugrim

"The Spell Begins to Break"
1. Sacks, ham, tea, sugar, matches, loaves of bread, six clean handkerchiefs
2. A cave, an old hiding-place for beavers in bad times
3. Father Christmas
4. It meant the Queen's magic is weakening
5. All: a tray with 5 cups and saucers, a bowl of lump sugar, a jug of cream, a piping hot teapot
   Mrs Beaver: sewing machine
   Mr. Beaver: Dam fixed and finished and a new sluice gate fitted
   Peter: shield and sword
   Susan: bow and arrows, horn
   Lucy: diamond cordial and dagger

"Aslan is Nearer"
1. Bread and water
2. The snow
3. she turned them into stone
4. Spring/Thaw
5. Tied his hands and made him walk

"Peter's First Battle"
1. An old, large slab of stone supported by four upright stones covered with engravings of strange letters of an unknown language
2. Dryads, naiads, centaurs, a unicorn, a man-headed bull, a pelican, an eagle, a dog and two leopards
3. The castle, Cair Paravel
4. Susan blew her horn
5. Killed the wolf
6. Clean his sword

"Deep Magic from the Dawn of Time"
1. Kill Edmund
2. An old tree-stump and a fair-sized boulder
3. She had to leave her wand by the great oak
4. The Stone Table, the World Ash Tree, the sceptre of the Emperor-Beyond-Sea, and the fire-stones of the Secret Hill
5. Narnia will be overturned and perish in fire and

THE CHRONICLES OF NARNIA
Comprehension Question Answers

water
6. Aslan's roar

"The Triumph of the Witch"
1. The Fords of Beruna
2. Susan and Lucy
3. The girls to lay their hands on his mane
4. Ogres, Wolves, bull-headed men, spirits of evil trees and poisonous plants, Cruels, Hags, Incubuses, Wraiths, Horrors, Efreets, Sprites, Orknies, Wooses, Ettins, Dwarves, Apes (and Spectres, Vultures, Bats)
5. Shaved Aslan
6. To kill Aslan instead of Edmund

"Deeper Magic from before the Dawn of Time"
1. Set off to war
2. Muzzle
3. Mice
4. Sunrise
5. Licked her forehead
6. When a willing victim who had committed no treachery was killed in a traitor's stead, the Table would crack and Death itself would start working backwards.
7. Gave a terrible roar
8. The Witch's castle
9. Aslan jumped/flew over the walls

"What Happened about the Statues"
1. A tiny streak of flame that creeps along the edge of a piece of newspaper when lit by a match
2. The giant
3. Mr. Tumnus the Faun
4. He destroyed the gate, two towers and a bit of wall to make an opening for everyone to pass through
5. Her handkerchief
6. A lion, a sheep-dog
7. Peter and Edmund and all the rest of Aslan's army fighting desperately against the Witch's horrible army. C. S. Lewis was once asked by a girl what happened to the merry-makers who were turned to stone. He replied, "I thought people would take it for granted that Aslan would put it all right. I see now I should have said so."
8. Peter

"The Hunting of the White Stag"
1. Edmund
2. Aslan wanted her to tend to the other wounded but she wanted to wait to see Edmund improve
3. Knighted him
4. Aslan provided the food
5. Cair Paravel
6. A wonderful hall with an ivory roof that had a western door hung with peacock feathers and an eastern door that opened right onto the sea
7. "Once a king or queen in Narnia, always a king or queen."
8. Mermen and mermaids
9. "He's wild, you know. Not like a tame lion."
10. Answers will vary. Among the things they did was destroy the remnants of the Witch's army, made good laws, kept the peace, prohibited unneccesary logging of good trees, kept young dwarfs and satyrs out of school, stopped busybodies, encouraged people to "live and let live," drove back the fierce giants in the North, formed treaties and alliances with other countries, and grew into adults (not grown-ups!).
11. White Stag
12. The same day and hour they had gone into the wardrobe to hide.
13. The missing coats

THE HORSE AND HIS BOY
"How Shasta Set Out on His Travels"
1. The Golden Age—during the reigns of High King Peter, King Edmund and Queens Susan and Lucy
2. He was a fisherman
3. He was a dark-skinned man with a curled crimson beard who wore a spiked helmet wrapped in a turban, chain mail, a scimitar, a round studded shield and a gold armband
4. Shasta
5. In the year the Tisroc took the throne, on a moonlit night, the fisherman could not sleep. While walking by the shore, he heard a weak cry and discovered a little boat bearing an infant and a dead man. Arsheesh took the child.
6. Shasta had always felt bad that he was unable to generate any love for Arsheesh
7. Run away to the North
8. With his knees
9. Breehy-hinny-brinny-hoohy-hah

THE CHRONICLES OF NARNIA
Comprehension Question Answers

"A Wayside Adventure"
1. He said it was booty, spoil
2. Bree rolled on his back on the ground/ he was worried that it was a bad habit he had picked up that Narnian horses did not practice
3. They were the Tisroc's wars and he had fought in them as a slave
4. Weeks and weeks
5. A long snarling roar from a lion
6. Another lion roar
7. It was just as bad as being caught by the lion, since he would be hung for horse-stealing
8. One great, shaggy and terrible lion
9. She was a talking horse and the Tarkaan was actually a young girl, both of whom were also running away
10. Second cousins once removed
11. Tell stories

"At the Gates of Tashbaan"
1. The betrothed of Aravis, Ahoshta was an old humpbacked man, not of royal blood, who through flattery and evil counsel worked his way up to being first in line to be the next Grand Vizier
2. Her horse spoke up and urged her not to.
3. Offer secret sacrifices to Zardeenah, Lady of the Night and of Maidens in the company of one of her servant girls
4. She drugged her drink
5. She posted a counterfeit letter to her father, supposedly from Ahoshta saying they had married immediately and he should bring her dowry to the home of Ahoshta
6. She would be beaten
7. The Tombs of the Ancient Kings
8. Hwin's plan was to cut their tails, roll in the mud and disguise the children as beggars then walk right through the city
9. Having their tails cut

"Shasta Falls in with the Narnians"
1. She didn't like going into the city as a beggar—she should have been carried in on a litter with slaves and soldiers round about her
2. Using his master's saddle-horse for pack work
3. Shasta was forced to the front of the crowd, then the Narnians grabbed him, accused him of being their missing runaway
4. Prince Corin of Archenland

5. Mr. Tumnus
6. Tumnus said that Shasta looked dazed and had been overexposed to the sun
7. Queen Susan was visiting Prince Rabadash to consider his offer of marriage
8. Three Weeks
9. Queen Susan had seen Prince Rabadash in his own home, and he had turned out, to quote King Edmund, "a proud, bloody, luxurious, cruel and self-pleasing tyrant."

"Prince Corin"
1. When Rabadash would learn of Susan's denial of marriage, Edmund thought they would become prisoners
2. The Raven discussed two ways to cross the great desert.
3. Moles planted an orchard—likely the same orchard which the children benefited from when they returned to aide Prince Caspian
4. Invite the Prince to a great banquet aboard the Narnian galleon
5. Lobsters, salad, stuffed snipe, a chicken liver dish, melons, frozen treats and white wine
6. The suit of armor he was to receive on his next birthday, a knighthood, the Summer Festival, dances and bonfires on Dancing Lawn and possibly getting to see Aslan
7. A porcelain vase being broken
8. Prince Corin
9. A boy in the street had made a joke at Queen Susan's expense
10. Go to King Lune and tell him that Shasta is a friend of Corin's

"Shasta Among the Tombs"
1. About twelve massive stone structures resembling narrow beehives, each with a low arched doorway opening into blackness
2. Jackals
3. The beast roared and then seemed to turn out to be a large green-eyed cat
4. He muttered to himself that he had once thrown stones at a half-starved stray cat
5. He had a short swim
6. He thought the others might have been to the tombs then left without him
7. Bree and Hwin appeared but without Aravis

THE CHRONICLES OF NARNIA
Comprehension Question Answers

"Aravis in Tashbaan"
1. She made eye contact with Lasaraleen
2. They had stayed at the same houses and been to the same parties before Lasaraleen was married
3. She had a new dress she wished people to see
4. He was in the city looking for Aravis
5. Though she thought the men "lovely," she did not find Queen Susan very pretty
6. Lasaraleen was a better talker than a listener, giggled often, and was primarily interested in clothes, parties and gossip
7. Aravis' betrothed had three palaces, one on Lake Ilkeen, possessing "ropes of pearls". . . and . . . "baths of asses' milk"
8. There was a big banquet that night
9. "Wait for him, of course"
10. The Tisrcoc, Prince Rabadash, and Ahoshta the Grand Vizier

"In the House of the Tisroc"
1. The Tisroc persuaded Rabadash that the Narnians had probably moved round the point for a better anchorage
2. Ahoshta quoted a poet's proverb to the Prince about reason extinguishing the flames of love
3. Narnia had, until recently, been covered in ice and snow making it an unattractive land to conquer. Also, the end of this enchantment was credited to powerful incantations by the Pevensies
4. Attacking Narnia, due to Aslan, was a "dark and doubtful enterprise" which the Tisroc did not wish to embark on because he did not want to put his hand out farther than he could draw it back
5. Rabadash suggested a way to attack Narnia without any adverse consequences to the Tisroc if the plan would fail
6. If he could capture and keep Anvard, they would sit at the very gate of Narnia where they could slowly build up a great army with which to attack Narnia at a later date
7. Rabadash believed that Peter in his prudence would see great advantage to being allied to the Tisroc's house through marriage
8. Narnian poetry was concerned with love and war while Calormen poetry was more proverbial—full of useful maxims
9. Rabadash was beginning to get dangerous, as Calormen princes have in the past, so his early death would help insure that the Tisroc didn't come to an untimely death

"Across the Desert"
1. She would go into the hallway and scream—insuring that they both were caught and killed
2. Lasaraleen's dresses, house and life
3. Getting two hundred horse and horsemen watered, victualed, armed and saddled takes time
4. Shasta had no shoes to wear and the sand burned his feet
5. A large rock in the shadow of which they were able to take their lunch and water the horses
6. When the moon had risen that night
7. They fell asleep
8. Going by the river valley took longer
9. Bree wanted a snack
10. Hwin

"The Hermit of the Southern March"
1. The river called the Winding Arrow
2. What he thought was smoke, but was actually the army of Prince Rabadash
3. A lion
4. The Hermit was a tall, bearded man dressed in a robe the color of autumn leaves
5. He shouted twice at the lion, "Go home!"
6. A wide, perfectly circular enclosure protected by a high turf wall. In the wall were two arched doorways opposite one another and a pool in the center which was overshadowed by a huge, beautiful tree. A low, thatched, stone-roofed house and some goats were the only other things there
7. King Lune
8. Ten
9. Luck
10. Return to Calormen
11. His self-conceit

"The Unwelcomed Fellow Traveller"
1. His son, Prince Corin
2. The way he mounted the horse—Shasta had "a true horseman's seat"
3. Shasta did not know how to use the reins or spurs to urge the dumb horse on
4. All the booty—the women, the gold, the jewels, the weapons and the wine
5. He realized that a large Thing was walking beside him
6. There was only one lion responsible for all the encounters
7. No one is told any story but their own
8. "Myself"

9. They said that Aslan was a demon who went around in the shape of a lion
10. Shasta slipped out of his saddle and fell at the feet of Aslan

"Shasta in Narnia"
1. Aslan's huge pawprint
2. A Hedgehog
3. The Stag
4. Porridge, cream, coffee, hot milk, toast, bacon and eggs with mushrooms
5. Rogin
6. The flag was a red rampant lion on a green field
7. Human men and women, talking and non-talking horses, centaurs, bears, talking dogs, giants and dwarfs
8. Prince Corin has been commanded not to fight in the battle at Anvard
9. King Peter prohibited Lucy from carrying it commonly to wars
10. Corin
11. The dwarf, Thornbut's armor

"The Fight at Anvard"
1. He taught him how to use the reins for his horse
2. She was like an ordinary grown-up lady—she did not ride to war
3. Heavy, horrid, spiked knee-high boots
4. He hashed his left knuckles against someone else's armor
5. By looking into the pool under the spreading tree within his hermitage
6. A battering ram
7. His old master, Anradin
8. The great cats
9. King Lune, flanked by Dar and Darrin
10. "The bolt of Tash falls from above."

"How Bree Became a Wiser Horse"
1. He wanted his tail to grow back
2. His whiskers
3. Aslan eat her
4. He told Bree to touch and smell him. He showed him his paws, tail and whiskers
5. The scratches were the equal of those Aravis' stepmother gave to the servant girl Aravis had drugged
6. Shasta
7. Cor would save Archenland from the deadliest danger in which she ever lay

8. Lord Chancellor Bar
9. Talking horses were not ridden except during war
10. Rolled in the bracken

"Rabadash the Ridiculous"
1. Cor rushing at the lion to save Aravis
2. Queen Lucy
3. He referred to how he changed from being a traitor to a friend when they first came to Narnia
4. Aslan
5. He was changed into a donkey
6. Never go more than ten miles from the great temple in Tashbaan
7. Rabadash the Ridiculous
8. Fighting the two-headed giant Pire, turning him into stone and winning the hand of Lady Liln
9. The King was under the law and could not break it, and the law said that the first born must be king
10. He boxed a lapsed talking bear on the Narnian side of Stormness for thirty-three rounds
11. Ram the Great

PRINCE CASPIAN: THE RETURN TO NARNIA
"The Island"
1. One year
2. Susan
3. They were looking for a freshwater stream
4. They had finished eating the only food that they had brought with them
5. An entire orchard of apple trees and some ruins

"The Ancient Treasure House"
1. Roasted apples
2. The gold chess piece which Susan found
3. Lilygloves
4. She suggested that they look for the door to their old treasure chamber
5. Susan
6. Edmund used his flashlight
7. Their gifts from Father Christmas
8. Susan's horn—it was lost when they had returned to England while chasing the White Stag

"The Dwarf"
1. In the same way that no time had passed when they came back through the wardrobe having

THE CHRONICLES OF NARNIA
Comprehension Question Answers

been Kings and Queens for years—Narnian time flows differently from our time.
2. A boat with two soldiers and a dwarf on board
3. Hit one soldier's helmet with an arrow
4. The woods around Cair Paravel were said to be haunted
5. Edmund's hat
6. Caspian the Tenth, King of Narnia

"The Dwarf Tells of Prince Caspian"
1. King Miraz and Queen Prunaprismia
2. His nurse
3. Cornelius was short, fat, ugly, old and had a pointed silvery beard that fell to his waist. He was Caspian's Tutor.
4. Two planets that pass within one degree of each other once every two hundred years; Tarva the Lord of Victory and Alambil the Lady of Peace
5. It had six empty rooms, a long stair and a locked door between it and the rest of the castle's inhabitants
6. He was a half dwarf
7. The Golden Age of Narnia
8. They were afraid of Aslan and of the trees

"Caspian's Adventure in the Mountains"
1. Miraz disapproved of ships and the sea
2. Queen Prunaprismia had a baby
3. Miraz shot a few in hunting parties, sent many to fight the Northern giants, over a dozen were executed for treason, two were put away as madmen, and seven set sail into the Eastern Ocean, never to return.
4. Gold and the Horn of Queen Susan
5. A tree branch during a storm
6. Two dwarves and a badger—Nikabrik, Trumpkin and Trufflehunter
7. Nikabrik

"The People That Lived in Hiding"
1. The Bulgie Bears, Pattertwig, the Seven Brothers of Shuddering Wood, five Black dwarves, and Glenstorm, Reepicheep, Clodsley Shovel the Mole, the three Hardbiters, Camillo the Hare, Hoglestock the Hedgehog, and the fauns Mentius, Obentinus, Dumnus, Voluns, Voltinus, Girbius, Nimienus, Nausus, and Oscuns.
2. To watch a squirrel go to his store of nuts or to look as if you wanted to know.
3. Shirts of mail, helmet and sword
4. An ogre or two and a hag

5. war
6. Wake the trees
7. A wide level circle of grass, bordered with tall elms and a well

"Old Narnia in Danger"
1. They wanted to have the feast first
2. Doctor Cornelius
3. Pass his sword through his throat
4. Caspian's horse, Destrier
5. Aslan's How. The word "how" comes from an old Norse word for mound or cairn
6. Aslan's How had room for all of their supplies and the galleries and caves would provide a place for retreat for all, except the giant
7. Blowing Queen Susan's horn
8. Aslan's How, Lantern Waste, or Cair Paravel
9. Sunrise sometimes had an effect in the operations of White Magic

"How They Left the Island"
1. The Horn of Susan was blown at the same time they were drawn into Narnia
2. Trumpkin risked a short cut across open country
3. Since the Pevensies were children he thought they would be no help in the war
4. Edmund asked Trumpkin to engage in a fencing match with him
5. Edmund disarmed the Dwarf using an old trick his fingers remembered—the Narnian air had been at work on him and all his old battle skills returned to him
6. An archery match with Susan
7. Healed his wound with a drop from her cordial
8. Dear Little Friend
9. The great ship had a swan's head at her prow and swan's wings which came back to the ship's midpoint, silk sails and musicians in the rigging

"What Lucy Saw"
1. She called out to the trees to wake the dryads and hamadryads, only to feel that she had spoken too soon or too late or had said something wrong.
2. A bear
3. If perhaps one day in our world men started going wild on the inside but still looked like men so one would never know which were which.
4. Aslan
5. To go down instead of up, as Aslan had instructed her to do.

THE CHRONICLES OF NARNIA
Comprehension Question Answers

"The Return of the Lion"
1. They fell under attack from Miraz's archers
2. Roasted Apples wrapped in bear meat
3. The trees
4. Aslan
5. Not because Aslan had grown, but because each year she grew, she would find Aslan bigger
6. Lucy buried her head in Alsan's mane and magically strength flowed into her
7. Peter unexpectedly agreed right away then rolled over to sleep again, Susan woke up then told Lucy (in her most "grown-up voice) that she had been dreaming and should go back to sleep, and Edmund was grumpy but went along with Lucy

"The Lion Roars"
1. The High King
2. Fixing her eyes on Aslan
3. After Aslan took a drink from the river, he turned his head to face them
4. Listening to her fears
5. Aslan pounced on him, carried him in his mouth like a ball, then shook him and threw him up into the air
6. Aslan roared
7. Bacchus, Sileneus and his donkeys and wild girls
8. Vines and grapes

"Sorcery and Sudden Vengeance"
1. Miraz attacked almost as soon as Trumpkin had left
2. He felt it had failed them
3. The White Witch
4. Aslan had not really come back to life and his absence in the old stories so soon after the Pevensies established their reign was confirmation of his death
5. The beavers
6. She said that witches never really die—you could always get them back.
7. A Hag and a Wer-wolf
8. Nikabrik, the Hag and the Wer-wolf were killed/ Caspian was bitten.

"The High King in Command"
1. Challenge Miraz to single combat
2. The day would then be filled with sending heralds back and forth, inspection of Miraz's army by Peter and strengthening their position.
3. Greenroof the 28th, in the first year of Caspian the Tenth
4. A coup—they plotted to push Miraz into accepting the challenge so he would either win outright, or die, and then they would take charge over Narnia
5. Whether Miraz ought to hazard their advantage by accepting the wager
6. Miraz called Glozelle a coward
7. Bears had the right to supply one marshall of the lists
8. The bear would suck his paw
9. Humans are afraid of mice, so Reepicheep's prescence might abate the edge of Miraz's courage

"How All Were Very Busy"
1. Dryads, Hamadryads and Silvans
2. "Huge people—beautiful people—like gods and goddesses and giants."
3. Peter's wrist was sprained by the rim of his shield
4. They shouted out that Peter had treacherously stabbed Miraz in the back and called Telmar to arms
5. Glozelle
6. The mice jabbed the enemy's feet with their tiny blades and if the enemy fell from hopping about, the mice would then finish them off.
7. The trees
8. Bacchus and his people caused great vines to grow up and tear down the bridge
9. Miss Prizzle's classroom was destroyed, Gwendolen was relieved of uncomfortable clothes and joined the Maenads, farm animals joyfully joined them, a cross man was turned into a tree, pig-like boys were turned into pigs while their school mistress joined Aslan's band, and healed "Auntie"

"Aslan Makes a Door in the Air"
1. Caspian said that he did not feel fit to take up the Kingship
2. His tail
3. Peepiceek and the other mice were prepared to cut off their own tails if Reepicheep went without
4. They were put under lock and key in Beruna and given beef and beer
5. Their wild dance provided food for everyone
6. Gazed with joy on the Moon
7. A doorway from nowhere to nowhere
8. Pirates
9. They are not coming back to Narnia
10. His new torch—his flashlight

THE CHRONICLES OF NARNIA
Comprehension Question Answers

THE VOYAGE OF THE DAWN TREADER
"The Picture in the Bedroom"
1. Eustace Clarence Scrubb
2. Professor Kirke/America
3. A picture of a single masted ship with a dragon head prow, gilded wings on a green hull and purple sail
4. She kicked off her shoes and kept her eyes open and mouth shut
5. Caspian
6. He got sick
7. Hot spiced wine
8. Hug him
9. A tiny room with a window, decorated with painted panels representing birds, beasts, vines and crimson dragons

"On Board the 'Dawn Treader'"
1. Lord Drinian
2. Three years
3. Revillian, Bern, Argoz, Mavramorn, Octesian, Restimar, Rhoop
4. Aslan's Country, a dryad
5. Sweet waves
6. To marry the duke's daughter
7. A drop from her diamond cordial
8. On a shelf inside the dragon head
9. Swung him around by the tail
10. Scrubb's school didn't have corporal punishment

"The Lone Islands"
1. Lucy
2. They were pirates and slavers/kidnappers
3. 150 crescents
4. He fell in love and married
5. Gumpas
6. A direct attack on Pug's ship
7. The non-existant Narnian fleet

"What Caspian Did There"
1. Friends of Bern and honest people warned the night before
2. A cask of wine be opened and the health of the king drunk to
3. Tribute
4. The abolishment of the slave trade
5. Eustace
6. Reconditioned in drydock, watered and victualled for a twenty-eight day sail

"The Storm and What Came of It"
1. Nearly three weeks
2. Playing chess
3. Twelve days
4. The mast, one sailor, the hens and two casks of water
5. Reepicheep
6. Nine
7. Two
8. To avoid work/ "have a good long sleep"
9. Loneliness
10. Thick fog

"The Adventures of Eustace"
1. After a second helping of roast goat
2. Dragon
3. He had "read none of the right books."
4. The death of the dragon
5. Thunderstorm/raining so hard
6. Treasure
7. A jewel-encrusted bracelet
8. Rhince had said it would be "a good riddance" if Eustace had been killed by wild beasts
9. A pain in his left arm
10. The brute's (dragon) mate
11. Large and hot
12. Sleeping on a dragon's hoard thinking greedy dragonish thoughts
13. He realized he wanted friends and that being a dragon cut him off from the human race
14. Fresh dragon
15. He found that he could fly
16. Eating Eustace
17. Reepicheep
18. Her diamond cordial

"How the Adventure Ended"
1. Octesian
2. Revictualling the ship, tearing up a tree to serve as a new mast, being a hot-water bottle, providing flights around the island for people
3. Six
4. Answers will vary
5. It was hung on a little projection in the rock above the inscription which Caspian had caused to be carved

THE CHRONICLES OF NARNIA
Comprehension Question Answers

"Two Narrow Escapes"
1. A coracle and paddle.
2. Green and vermillian with purple blotches and shellfish attached periodically/horse-shaped head without ears/enormous eyes and a double row of fish-like teeth
3. He jumped up on the bulwark and hacked at the serpent with a sword
4. It broke off the carved stern
5. A Narnian sword-hilt
6. A hunting spear
7. King Caspian ordered King Edmund to keep the pool a secret
8. Aslan
9. He was low on tobacco

"The Island of Voices"
1. Park-like grounds, manicured like a great English house
2. A little stone in her shoe
3. Get between the landing party and the boat, then catch the landing party as they tried to put out to sea
4. "Machinery"—a water pump appearing to move up and down by itself
5. Fifty
6. an uglifying spell
7. To go upstairs in the magician's house and cast the spell which would make them visible

"The Magician's Book"
1. Huge grasshoppers or frogs
2. The conversations consisted almost entirely of agreements
3. A carved and panelled hallway full of curiously painted doors, a bearded mirror
4. She had to stand with her back to a door which she couldn't shut
5. A cure for warts/toothaches/cramps, a spell for taking a swarm of bees, how to find buried treasure, how to remember things forgotten, how to forget things you want to forget, how to tell whether anyone is speaking the truth, how to call up (or prevent) fog/snow/sleet/rain, how to produce enchanted sleeps, how to give a man an ass's head, a beautifying spell, a spell to know what your friends thought about you, a spell for refreshment, a spell to make things hidden visible
6. The face of Aslan appeared
7. Marjorie told Anne Featherstone that Lucy is not a "bad little kid in her way" but that she was pretty tired of her by the end of the school term
8. A cup, a sword, a tree and a green hill
9. Aslan
10. Aslan abides by his own rules
11. Eavesdropping
12. Aslan would tell Lucy the story from the book for years and years

"The Dufflepuds Made Happy"
1. A barefoot old man with a long beard wrapped in a red robe, crowned with a chaplet of oak leaves and supported with a carved staff
2. Sir Trumpkin the Dwarf, Knight of the Order of the Lion
3. It made him sleepy
4. Wine and bread
5. Refusing to get water from the stream that runs by the garden
6. Washing plates and knives before dinner, planting boiled potatoes, moving all the milk out of the dairy to keep it away from the cat
7. Astrolabe: instrument once used to calculate the altitude of stars
   Orrery: A mechanical model which shows how the planets revolve around the sun
   Chronoscope: A device used to measure time in decimals
   Poesimeter: An imaginary device used to measure the meter of poems
   Choriambus: An imaginary device used to measure choriambs (a metrical foot consisting of four syllables: long, short, short, long)
   Theodolite: A surveying device used to measure horizontal and vertical angles
8. He taught them how to carve rude paddles for themselves so that they could use their feet like little boats
9. With Drinian's help he had magical maps drawn up
10. He magically mended the stern which had been broken off by the sea serpent

"The Dark Island"
1. Twelve days/ playing chess
2. Adventure and honor
3. He was measuring the depth of the water so the ship wouldn't run aground in the Darkness
4. The island where dreams come true
5. She called on Aslan for help
6. An albatross

THE CHRONICLES OF NARNIA
Comprehension Question Answers

7. Lord Rhoop
8. To never let anyone ask him about what he saw on the Dark Island

"The Three Sleepers"
1. A wide, unroofed oblong space flagged with smooth stones and surrounded by grey pillars
2. The last three lords
3. A beautiful girl, tall and dressed in a long blue sleeveless garment whose yellow hair fell down her back
4. One of the lords grabbed the Knife of Stone— a thing which was not right for him to touch
5. The Knife of Stone—sharp as steel, cruel and ancient looking—used by the White Witch to kill Aslan
6. Reepicheep
7. Sleeping Beauty
8. The prince may not kiss the princess until he had broken the enchantment

"The Beginning of the End of the World"
1. Sang to the rising sun
2. Birds/lay what looked like a shining piece of fruit or a live coal (actually a fire-berry) on the Old Man's tongue
3. They must sail to the World's End or as near as possible and then leave one of their company to sail into the utter east to never return
4. A star
5. He was a star set to govern the Duffers as a punishment
6. That they'd have to row all the way back to Narnia
7. Gold or land enough to make him rich for the rest of his life and the title "Dawn Treader" which would be bequeathed to all his descendants
8. Dreamless sleep
9. He can't bear mice
10. Caspian wanted to speak with Ramandu's daughter upon his return

"The Wonders of the Last Sea"
1. They needed less sleep, the sun was much larger, and the water was quite clear
2. Their naked bodies were the color of ivory and their hair dark purple. They were unlike merpeople in that they did not have fish tails but instead rode large sea horses.
3. He discovered that the water was sweet, that is,

fresh water—not salt water
4. The water made it that they didn't need food and they could look directly into the sun
5. They may just pour right over the edge of the world
6. Our world is round but the world Narnia is in is flat

"The Very End of the World"
1. Lilies
2. The current was only about forty feet wide
3. Caspian wished to abdicate and continue on into the utter East
4. Ulysses
5. Reepicheep, Eustace and the Pevensies were to go on while the Dawn Treader was to head back to Narnia
6. A wall of water—a long wave behind which they saw Aslan's country
7. He floated in his coracle over the wave into Aslan's country
8. A lamb roasting breakfast over a fire
9. There are ways into his country from all worlds
10. He told her that he is in our world too, but goes by a different name
11. She married Caspian and became a great queen as well as a mother and grandmother to great kings

THE SILVER CHAIR
"Behind the Gym"
1. She had been the recipient of bullying
2. Scrubb had changed since the previous term—he was standing up instead of sucking up to the bullies
3. He had been out of our world, into a place where animals can talk—a fairy tales sort of place
4. Scrubb thought Aslan wouldn't like them—it would appear as if one could make Aslan do things for them
5. Hold out their arms to the east with their palms-facing down and call out to Aslan
6. Through the door in the high stone wall which ran around the perimeter of the school
7. Riotous, musical birdsong against a backdrop of immense silence
8. Scrubb turned white from seeing that they were on the edge of a high precipice
9. While struggling with Jill, Scrubb lost his balance and fell over the cliff
10. A lion

THE CHRONICLES OF NARNIA
Comprehension Question Answers

"Jill is Given a Task"
1. Remembering Scrubb's scream as he fell
2. She was thirsty
3. He said that he had swallowed up girls, boys, women, men, kings, emperors, cities and realms
4. Aslan told her that he had called her and Scrubb out of our world
5. They would only have called if Aslan had first been calling to them
6. To seek the lost Narnian prince until they are able to return him to his father, have died, or have gone back into their own world
7. 1. Eustace must greet his old friend as soon as he sets foot in Narnia. 2. Journey to the ruined city of the ancient giants. 3. Do what is instructed on the writing they find on a stone in the ruined city. 4. The prince is identified as the first person they meet who requests that something be done in the name of Aslan.
8. The signs would not appear as she expects them to and the air and her mind were clear in Aslan's country while they would not be in Narnia
9. Recite them when she wakes in the morning, lies down at night and wakes in the middle of the night
10. On the breath of Aslan

"The Sailing of the King"
1. Glimfeather the Owl
2. Caspian the Tenth, the Seafarer
3. Trumpkin the Dwarf
4. That they had come to look for the lost prince
5. The Experiment House did not teach the children who Adam and Eve were
6. A round room up in one of the castle's turrets which possessed a bath sunk in the floor, a flat hearth and low-hanging lamp
7. Eustace did not talk with his old friend the King
8. Aslan must have blown Jill faster to make up for lost time
9. Soups, pavenders, venison, peacocks, pies, ices and jellies, fruits, nuts, fruit drinks and wine
10. The Horse and his Boy

"A Parliament of Owls"
1. He was the King's man and would have nothing to do with a plot against the King.
2. The King told him not to allow any other champions to get lost looking for the prince because Narnia had already lost more than thirty champions (including knights, centaurs, giants, etc.).
3. Caspian had never forgotten his voyage to the world's end and wanted to go there again.
4. Because they were owls, they found meeting during the day an unnatural practice
5. Rilian and Caspian's Queen rode north to go maying with squires and ladies. Rilian and the party left the Queen to have a nap, during which a green serpent bit her.
6. A beautiful woman wrapped in a thin garment of green
7. Caspian rushed upon Lord Drinian with a battle-axe to kill him, but instead embraced him and wept
8. Mention of the ruined city of the giants
9. The Marsh-wiggles

"Puddleglum"
1. Long legs and arms ending in webbed fingers and feet, a torso not much bigger than a dwarf's. Long thin face with sunken cheeks, sharp nose, no beard and reed-like locks of "hair."
2. It would probably rain, snow, fog or thunder. The children likely would not get any sleep. They would forget his name, he would not catch any eels, the children would not like his food, the wood would be wet and if it were able to be lit—rain would douse it.
3. They had said he was too flighty, did not take life seriously enough, and was too full of "bobance and bounce"
4. Sailing east on the Dawn Treader
5. Puddleglum's snoring

"The Wild Waste Lands of the North"
1. Giants
2. The giants were aiming at a cairn to the right of the travellers and since they are such bad shots, they were likely to hit Puddleglum, Scrubb and Jill
3. The "howling and blubbering and boo-hooing" of the giants
4. The giant laughed at them
5. A knight whose armor and horse were completely black and a lady wearing a dazzling green dress sitting side-saddle on a white horse
6. She of the Green Kirtle salutes them and has sent two fair Southern children for the Autumn Feast
7. A skeleton, someone invisible, or no one at all
8. Whether or not they should go to Harfang

THE CHRONICLES OF NARNIA
Comprehension Question Answers

9. The children had to promise to not reveal that they were looking for Prince Rilian or that they were from Narnia
10. The Lady of the Green Kirtle putting into their minds the beds and baths of Harfang

"The Hill of the Strange Trenches"
1. A snowstorm had descended upon them
2. Puddleglum asked which of Aslan's signs was next
3. They saw the lights of Harfang
4. Their blue faces
5. A giant silver salt cellar
6. Girls were not taught how to curtsey at the Experiment House

"The House of Harfang"
1. Broke down and cried
2. Cock-a-leekie soup, hot roast turkey, steamed pudding, roast chestnuts and fruit
3. Toting in oversized, garish toys
4. Aslan
5. The Ruinous City and the inscription, "UNDER ME"
6. Puddleglum imagined that the Lady of the Green Kirtle intended that the children and the Marshwiggle forget about Prince Rilian
7. Sneak out by daylight
8. Gay
9. They were going out hunting
10. She wanted to know if the children were to be allowed to attend the feast on the following evening

"How They Discovered Something Worth Knowing"
1. The scullery door opened out through the outer wall so you didn't have to pass over the courtyard or pass the great gatehouse
2. He heard that the venison they were eating was from a Narnian stag
3. A cookbook containing—among other receipes—instructions for the best way to cook Mallard, Man and Marsh-wiggle
4. Their bright colors drew attention to the children and they were much too thin to provide protection against the cold
5. If the children escaped, there would be "no man-pies tomorrow."
6. They filled the opening with rocks
7. They slid down a slope of small stones and rubbish
8. His tinder box

"Travels Without the Sun"
1. The Warden of the Marches of Underland
2. Few returned to the sunlit lands.
3. The earthmen were so sad that Puddleglum thought they were the ones to teach him to take a serious view of life
4. Father Time
5. The Black Knight
6. Scrubb bursting out about how mean the Queen of Underland was to send them to Harfang to be eaten
7. UNDER ME is part of a longer inscription which read, "Though under Earth and throneless now I be, Yet, while I lived, all Earth was under me."
8. Puddleglum trusted that Aslan was there when the inscription was cut and foresaw its impact on this future adventure
9. She was of a divine race which doesn't age or die
10. The Queen of Underland's hand in marriage

"In the Dark Castle"
1. After becoming furious and wild, he was changed into a great serpent
2. Inspecting the diggings
3. It would hinder his deliverance from the enchantment he was under
4. A curious silver chair
5. ". . . by the great Lion, by Aslan himself, I charge you—". The Knight fulfills the final sign.
6. He destroyed the chair
7. Prince Rilian, son of Caspian X
8. Ten years

"The Queen of the Underland"
1. He renounced the Queen's plan for Rilian to lead an attack on the Overworld as plain villainy; he declared his identity as Rilian the son of Caspian the Seafarer and required safe conduct out of the Queen's realm
2. Threw a handful of green powder into the fire and began playing a musical instrument
3. She proposed that Narnia was just a dream
4. The sun
5. Aslan
6. The Queen told them that everything they "remembered" was make-believe copies of things from her world
7. He stamped out the fire
8. She transformed into a loathsome serpent, green as poison

THE CHRONICLES OF NARNIA
Comprehension Question Answers

9. Hacked off her head
10. Rilian deduced that the serpent which killed the daughter of Ramandu was the Lady of the Green Kirtle.

"Underland Without the Queen"
1. With magic spells she had set it that if she would die, the one who had killed her would be burned, drowned or buried five minutes later
2. It had changed from black to silver with a red lion across it
3. Kneel and kiss the likeness of Aslan
4. Coalback and Snowflake the horses
5. When Rilian told him that he had killed the Queen

"The Bottom of the World"
1. The Land of Bism
2. The Witch had called them up by magic
3. There was no roof—only sky
4. A stained-glass window and a tropical sun at mid-day
5. White-hot, eloquent and witty salamanders
6. To refuse the adventures of Bism would be an impeachment to their honor
7. Rubies were picked in bunches, diamonds were squeezed into juice
8. The lamps on the road going out
9. It saved on funeral expenses

"The Disappearance of Jill"
1. Jill being pulled through the hole out of Puddleglum's hands
2. The Great Snow Dance
3. He was brandishing his sword and making lunges at anyone who came near him
4. They carted away the diggings in little barrows
5. He wanted to hear what bad news there was (forest fires, dragons, etc.)
6. The "Northern Witches always mean the same thing, but in every age they have a different plan for getting it."

"The Healing of Harms"
1. Sausages, hot chocolate, roast potatoes, roast chestnuts, baked apples with cores filled with raisins, and ices
2. Scrambled eggs and toast
3. Feeding both the man-stomach and the horse-stomach was a huge undertaking

4. Aslan had told him to return
5. They were allowed to ride on the back of centaurs
6. The properties of plants and herbs, the influences of the planets and the nine names of Aslan
7. After blessing Rilian, Caspian died
8. The funeral music for Caspian
9. To find a thorn and drive it into the paw of Aslan
10. She got a job in Parliment where she lived happily ever after
11. She wore them to a fancy dress ball the next holidays
12. It was left open and used for boating parties on the cool, dark underground sea

THE LAST BATTLE
"By Caldron Pool"
1. Shift was very clever
2. A lion's skin
3. Bury it
4. Making alterations in the skin so it would fit the Donkey
5. Aslan the Great Lion
6. Tricking Narnians was good because with Shift to "advise" Puzzle, they could set things right in Narnia
7. The lack of oranges and bananas and the need for more sugar
8. A warning that Shift's plot was dreadfully wrong
9. Shift was "just going to say" Aslan would send a thunderclap if it was his will that Puzzle impersonate the Lion

"The Rashness of the King"
1. They had saved each other's lives
2. Aslan was in Narnia
3. The stars foretold disasterous events and that the news of Aslan being in Narnia was a lie
4. The stories said that Aslan was "not a tame lion"
5. Forty trees had been cut down in Lantern Waste
6. Her tree was cut down
7. A score of men-at-arms, a score of talking dogs, ten dwarf archers, a Leopard or so and Stonefoot the Giant
8. Half the crowd were Calormen
9. It was a Talking Horse
10. They beheaded and gored the two Calormen who were whipping the horse

THE CHRONICLES OF NARNIA
Comprehension Question Answers

"The Ape in Its Glory"
1. The possibility that Aslan had come but was not like the Aslan long believed in and longed for
2. Jewel had a rope halter placed around his neck while Tirian's hands were bound behind his back and his gold circlet was stolen from him
3. Uglier than ever before, Shift was wearing a poor-fitting scarlet jacket which had been made for a dwarf, jeweled slippers on (and off) his hind paws, a paper crown on his head and nuts in his mouth. He added to this the king's sword, hung round his neck
4. He demanded twice the nuts from the squirrels by sunset the following day
5. He claimed to be a man instead of an ape
6. A steady supply of oranges and bananas, roads, big cities, schools, offices, whips, muzzles, saddles, cages, kennels and prisons
7. Shift said Tash is Aslan: Aslan is Tash
8. The cat, Ginger
9. He said the Ape lied like a Calormen

"What Happened That Night"
1. He couldn't wipe away the trickle of blood from his lip and it tickled
2. Wine and cheese, oat-cakes with fresh butter
3. He recalled Shift's nonsensical statement about Tash and Aslan being the same
4. If Aslan would not come himself, would he please send the children from beyond the world
5. A lighted room where seven people sat around a table, having just finished their meal. There was an old man and old woman, two young men and a young woman and a young boy and girl—all dressed in the oddest kind of clothes.
6. Peter the High King

"How Help Came to the King"
1. Eustace and Jill
2. Nearly a week
3. Two boiled egg sandwiches, two cheese sandwiches and two "paste" sandwiches
4. A guard tower in Lantern Waste
5. For the enjoyment of talking over Narnian things and because he had a feeling they were wanted in Narnia
6. Dressed as workmen so if anyone asked they would say they were working on the drains
7. Aslan delivered them immediately following a "frightful jerk and a noise" from the train they

were riding
8. A liquid for disguising themselves as Calormen with southern armour to match
9. Archery
10. A firkin or so of good wine

"A Good Night's Work"
1. Sword fight using a scimitar
2. Rescue Jewel
3. Spear-Head
4. Sitting against the stable with his mouth stuffed with grass and chin tied up
5. She freed the false Aslan, Puzzle
6. Decapitate the Donkey
7. He was eager to show the truth of the Ape's vile plot

"Mainly About Dwarfs"
1. They killed them while the dwarfs handled the other two of the Tisroc's men
2. Tirian said that Aslan was "not a tame lion."
3. The Dwarfs are for the Dwarfs
4. It caused people to stop believing in the real Aslan
5. Poggin the Dwarf
6. Grass, sugar and the care of hoofs
7. He said that Tirian was cursing Aslan when the Lion appeared in a flash of lightning, only to swallow up the King in one mouthful
8. Neither Tash nor Aslan truly exist

"What News the Eagle Brought"
1. Tash had the smell of death and the opacity of smoke. It was in the shape of a man with the head of a bird, four arms and talons instead of fingers
2. They couldn't be sure the animals and dwarfs would rally behind the King instead of just sitting and looking on at what would transpire
3. Jill assumed that there was always a great deal happening in Narnia
4. Swanwhite was so beautiful that when she looked into a forest pool her reflection would shine out of it like a star—day and night—for a year and a day afterward
5. King Gale delivered the islands from the threat of a dragon and the islanders gave the Lone Islands to Narnia in appreciation
6. Farsight the Eagle
7. Cair Paravel captured and flying the Tisoc's banner, Roonwit the Centaur lying dead

8. "remember that all worlds draw to an end and that a noble death is a treasure which no one is too poor to buy."

"The Great Meeting on Stable Hill"
1. Go back to Stable Hill, proclaim the truth and take what adventure Aslan sends
2. Go back to their world
3. They were in possesion of none of the magic needed to return to England
4. Being smashed in a British Railways accident
5. The Narnians suggested that they might hide out in the woods of the Western Waste like outlaws, then sweep the Calormen out of Narnia when the enemy got careless
6. He said that a Donkey had been seen wandering around the woods dressed in a lion skin pretending to be Aslan

"Who Will Go Into the Stable?"
1. Cut the lion skin off of Puzzle
2. Shift said that anyone may go in to the stable to see Tashlan
3. They must go in one at a time, Tashlan had been licking his lips since eating Tirian, and he had been growling all morning
4. "We are all between the paws of the true Aslan"
5. Ginger the Cat
6. Ginger turned into a dumb beast
7. Emeth
8. They began to close in around a talking Boar to make him go into the stable at scimitar-point

"The Pace Quickens"
1. 1) The Tarkaan jumped out of harm's way and called the Calormen and Narnians to his side
   2) The Ape was thrown into the stable and then from within the stable there was a blinding, greenish-blue flash followed by monsterous bird noises
   3) The Talking Dogs rushed to the side of the King
2. They feared for the wrath of Tashlan
3. Freeing the talking horses
4. Wraggle the Satyr and the Talking Bull
5. Because the "Dwarfs are for the Dwarfs"
6. The Dwarfs killed the Talking Horses
7. The answering drum of Calormen reinforcements
8. The eagle's attacks and Jill's arrows

"Through the Stable Door"
1. Eustace
2. He threw them into the "shrine of Tash"
3. The boar, the dogs and the unicorn would live (in bondage) if they gave themselves up—but the eagle, the children and the king were to be offered to Tash
4. Spears
5. He jumped back into the stable, taking the Tarkaan with him
6. He was banished in the name of Aslan and Aslan's great Father, the Emperor-over-the-sea
7. He was cleaned and dressed in fine Narnian clothes like that he wore for feasts at Cair Paravel
8. Lady Jill
9. "My sister Susan is no longer a friend of Narnia." Tirian's simple question of "Where is Queen Susan?" has been the source of much concern and debate since *The Last Battle* was published. One woman went so far as to write an apocryphal Chronicle entitled "The Centaur's Cavern" to explain how Susan gets back into Narnia. The first footnote under Susan's entry in *Companion of Narnia* is very helpful in understanding the meaning behind Susan's absence at the end of *The Last Battle*. Older students may wish to read John 6:37-40 and Aslan's last words at the coronation in *The Lion, The Witch and the Wardrobe*, then write a paragraph explaining why Susan *will* eventually join the others in Aslan's Country.

"How the Dwarfs Refuse to Be Taken In"
1. They followed Peter's suggestion to eat the fruit from a grove of trees nearby
2. They were on their way to Bristol
3. They felt unstiffened
4. Both held things inside which were bigger than the stable was outside
5. Ginger had seen Tash
6. Manure and thistles
7. A feast
8. The suspicion that the other Dwarfs had found better things to eat

THE CHRONICLES OF NARNIA
Comprehension Question Answers

"Night Falls on Narnia"
1. In the deep caves beneath the high moorlands beyond the River Shribble
2. The stars fell from the sky
3. Glittery with long hair, the appearance of burning silver, carrying spears like white-hot metal
4. They ceased to be talking animals and disappearded into the shadow of Aslan
5. The great joy of seeing alive all those he thought dead
6. "Further in and higher up!"
7. The Dragons and Great Lizards
8. He was told to shut the door—which he did, and locked it with a golden key
9. A Calormene

"Further Up and Further In"
1. He found it shameful that they would be entering Narnia disguised, using lies and trickery
2. Because Aslan and Tash are opposites—no deed which is not vile can be given to Tash
3. Emeth called himself a dog, using the word in a derogatory fashion
4. The land they were walking in was the real Narnia
5. "Bless me, what do they teach them at these schools!"
6. They could all run as fast as the Unicorn could gallop

"Farewell to Shadowlands"
1. The Great Waterfall by Caldron Pool
2. Lord Digory and Lady Polly had flown over the western Wilds when Narnia began
3. Reepicheep
4. A phoenix
5. Each circle you go in is larger than the last rather than smaller
6. Professor Kirk's old house
7. There was a real railway accident and they are all "dead"